Make Your Music Video and Put It Online

Robert Safir

Course Technology PTR

A part of Cengage Learning

COURSE TECHNOLOGY
CENGAGE Learning

Australia, Brazil, Japan, Korea, Mexico, Singapore, Spain, United Kingdom, United States

COURSE TECHNOLOGY
CENGAGE Learning

**Make Your Music Video
and Put It Online**
Robert Safir

**Publisher and General Manager,
Course Technology PTR:**
Stacy L. Hiquet

Associate Director of Marketing:
Sarah Panella

Manager of Editorial Services:
Heather Talbot

Marketing Manager:
Mark Hughes

Acquisitions Editor:
Orren Merton

Development Editor:
Orren Merton

Project Editors:
Sandy Doell, Kezia Endsley

Technical Reviewer:
Kenn Michael

Copy Editor:
Melba Hopper

Interior Layout:
Shawn Morningstar

Cover Designer:
Luke Fletcher

Indexer:
Katherine Stimson

Printed in the United States of America
1 2 3 4 5 6 7 11 10 09

For product information and technology assistance, contact us at

**Cengage Learning Customer and Sales Support,
1-800-354-9706**

For permission to use material from this text or product, submit all requests online at
cengage.com/permissions

Further permissions questions can be emailed to
permissionrequest@cengage.com

All trademarks are the property of their respective owners. All images © Cengage Learning unless otherwise noted.

Library of Congress Control Number: 2009924529

ISBN-13: 978-1-59863-997-1

ISBN-10: 1-59863-997-8

Course Technology, a part of Cengage Learning
20 Channel Center Street
Boston, MA 02210
USA

Cengage Learning is a leading provider of customized learning solutions with office locations around the globe, including Singapore, the United Kingdom, Australia, Mexico, Brazil, and Japan. Locate your local office at:
international.cengage.com/region

Cengage Learning products are represented in Canada by Nelson Education, Ltd.

For your lifelong learning solutions, visit **courseptr.com**
Visit our corporate website at **cengage.com**

I dedicate this book to the music makers,
the dreamers of dreams, and to the filmmakers,
who visualize those dreams for others to see and hear.
This book is also dedicated to my wife Lynne,
who was supportive throughout the writing of this book,
and to Marty, Margie, and Anthony, for being there for me
during the whole process...and to Betsy—even though she
couldn't be there—I could hear her encouraging meows
in my head.

Acknowledgments

A HUGE THANK YOU goes out to Orren Merton. He is a multi-dimensional, multifaceted, multitalented (and multimedia) guy with a great blend of left- and right-brain thinking. He was a big supporter for this book from day one and has been there with extremely thoughtful answers whenever questions arose.

Thanks also to the staff at Cengage Learning, especially the talented editors Kezia Endsley, Melba Hopper, and Kenn Michael, all masters of their craft.

This book never would have been completed without the strong support of my family, including my wife Lynne, brother Marty, sister-in-law Margie, and nephew, Anthony. Thanks for hanging in there with me!

Along my personal road in the music business, there have been many people who were either role models or mentors or just plain helpful, whether they knew it or not. Included in this group are the multitalented producer Curt Boetcher, the songwriting expert John Braheny, and the very wise Richard Bellis. Thank you for sharing your insights.

About the Author

ROBERT SAFIR began his career in the pro music biz at the tender age of 17, placing original songs with Top 40 artists The Standells and getting his own record deals as an artist, first with GNP Crescendo, and later, with ABC Records. Later, Robert founded Track Record Studios in Los Angeles, where he engineered or produced for The Association, Canned Heat, Brian Wilson, Chad Stuart, Lauren Wood, and others.

Robert became fascinated with film and learned all aspects of it, from camera to final edit. The combination of music with all forms of media has been the focus of his career, which has included the production of audio, film, video, and multimedia. He has always had a marketing bent, and has been a marketing communications manager or director at companies such as E-mu Systems, Digidesign, Microsoft, and Cisco Systems.

Robert is active in the music industry in a variety of ways. As an author, Robert has been staff writer for *Keyboard Magazine*, as well as writing articles for other industry pubs such as *Mix* magazine, *Songwriter, Cue,* and *The Hollywood Reporter.* He has also penned articles for *The Score*, a publication the Society of Composers and Lyricists (SCL), a highly respected organization. As a panelist, he has presented at The Computer Game Developer's Conference, AES (Audio Engineering Society), Mix '99, and California Lawyers for the Arts.

In addition to his film scores, some of Robert's recent works have aired on ABC Television, The Discovery Channel, E! Entertainment, The Biography Channel, BET, The Learning Channel, Spike TV, and others.

Table of Contents

PART II
Producing Your Video

Chapter 3
Music Video Cookbook: The Ingredients

Chapter 4
Choosing Your Production Methods

Chapter 9
Post-Production 105

PART III
Posting Your Masterpiece on the Internet

Chapter 10
Making Your Video Internet-Ready 129

Chapter 11
Evaluating Popular Online Sites. 137

Chapter 12
Working with iTunes Videos 151

Chapter 13

Appendix A

Introduction

WHY IS IT IMPORTANT TO GET YOUR music video on the Internet? It's not important at all—that is, unless you realize the tremendous advantages of using technology to successfully promote your band or yourself as an artist. It's not important unless you want to have a leg up on the competition. (You're not even in the competition if you're not creating your own promotional media.) It's not important unless you still believe in the old models of the music industry, replete with record companies, Top 40 charts, and radio as the primary means of reaching your audience.

In short, you're living in a brave new world of do-it-yourself music creation and distribution. At your disposal are music creation tools that would have been a dream—a utopia, an absolute nirvana—for a producer such as George Martin and those other four guys (The Beatles). Depending on the size of your budget, your video production can easily be at Internet-quality levels, and on the high end, it could be high definition, widescreen, and ready to show at a theater, let alone on the Internet. In this brave new world, there are fewer walls between you and your audience. As the Internet has democratized many aspects of our lives and leveled the playing field, it has also had a major impact on your ability to get heard, to get known, and to get ahead.

The Third Wave and the Age of the Prosumer

Long, long ago, in the twentieth century, there lived an author by the name of Alvin Toffler. More than "just" an author, Toffler became known as a "futurist" by the success of his well-known books, *Future Shock* and *The Third Wave*. Without getting into a full book report, one can summarize Toffler's thinking by the phrases he coined (or expanded upon): super-industrial society, the information age, electronic era, global village, and mass customization. Toffler has an uncanny ability to see into the future through the eyes of history, current trends, and the ways in which change interacts with other change.

Years ago, he was able to predict the evolution of the prosumer—a fusion between the producer and the consumer. Prosumers not only consume, but also produce—in small quantities or large. Prosumers can fill their own needs. Prosumers can utilize technologies to become more independent; they are less likely to need the corporation and more likely to be an innovator, entrepreneur, or even a maverick. Today's musicians, recording engineers, video editors, directors, and artists of all types are the ultimate prosumers. *You*, more than likely, are a prosumer.

Never before has such great power been in the hands of so many people through technological advances as it is today. This book focuses on the production of music, of music videos, and of Internet marketing—all of which are great examples of powerful technology in the hands of the individual. Combined, these disciplines comprise a new method of marketing in which you—the prosumer—have more control than ever before.

Music Marketing and Promotion in the Twenty-First Century

Just as the face of music production has changed, so has marketing and promotion. The standard marketing techniques that used to work in the music business no longer work with the "new rules." A large component of the new rules is that there are no rules.

The Old-School Approach

But before throwing out the baby with the bathwater, let's make sure we preserve some general marketing practices that seem to have worked in the last century as well as this one. The accepted guru in this department is Al Reis, whose books (such as *The 22 Immutable Laws of Marketing, Focus, The 11 Immutable Laws of Internet Marketing*, and many more) contain valuable marketing principles that are easy to understand and apply to marketing music videos on the Internet as well as they do to soap and cereal. These principles include positioning your product in the mind of the consumer, repositioning the competition, being first, being best (and, if possible, both), focusing on your strengths (and remaining focused), and the willingness to embrace change.

All of these concepts apply to you as much as they apply to Coca-Cola or Xerox or Federal Express. You are the product. You are the marketer. And you are also the distributor.

That's a lot of work for one person or a small group of people to handle, so, with this book, I hope you will be able to utilize the great concepts from classical marketing and throw in some new ones as well.

New School, New Rules

This is where other marketing techniques, such as guerilla marketing, viral marketing, and social marketing come in. *Guerilla marketing* relies less on big budgets and more on human psychology. It is unconventional marketing that focuses more on creating buzz, referrals, and inexpensive publicity. It advocates using new technologies as a tool to empower your business and promote your product.

Viral marketing is the reliance on word-of-mouth marketing, enhanced by personal and business networks, to increase brand awareness and other marketing objectives. This is where you will see promotions that utilize video clips, Flash media, and animation to increase the likelihood of spreading the word. Like guerilla marketing, it is unconventional and often very effective.

Social marketing has a variety of definitions, but in the context of this book, it refers to the utilization of social networks to convey the marketing message. These networks include well-known sites such as MySpace, Facebook, Friendster, Blogger, and a host of sites that focus on music or entertainment, such as iMeem and Bebo. At one time, these networks were the sole territory of cutting edge, new age, modern, hip geeks. Today, you will find major corporations (from the "old school") relying on social networks for unconventional marketing campaigns.

All of these marketing and promotion techniques have a place in the world of music and music videos, and they will be explored further in the discussion of posting your music video on the Internet.

Who Should Read This Book

If you've read this far, you're likely a good candidate for reading the rest of this book. If the idea of making your own music video and marketing it on the Internet gives you hope, goose bumps, and the thought that maybe there are other roads to the top of the mountain, you probably should read this book.

In terms of level of expertise, this book is designed for beginners or newcomers on one hand, but also should appeal to anyone who hasn't looked at the three main ingredients—namely, music creation, video production, and Internet marketing—as an integrated whole. There are concepts covered in this book in which the whole is greater than the sum of its parts. You may have experience in one or two of these areas, but all three taken together can make for a very successful marketing and promotional campaign and may spark ideas you haven't considered before.

You should also have some fundamental understanding of music creation and video production, and you need to know your way around the web. I will cover these topics, but not with the assumption that you've never used a computer or a sequencer or a video-editing program of some type. You are likely a songwriter or composer who has a sequencer and some virtual and/or real instruments and who knows how to create a song from writing to mixing. Now you're ready for the next step—making a music video and posting it on the Internet.

Who Shouldn't Read This Book

Don't read this book if you are planning to start from nothing and end up producing a broadcast-ready music video for VH1 or MTV. You probably should not read this book if you don't have some inherent talent, drive, or obsession with one or more of the three main ingredients (music creation, video production, or Internet marketing). But whatever the case, do what your inner voice tells you. And if that means you want to read it no matter what I say about the target audience, then go right ahead...and enjoy.

What to Expect by Reading This Book

This book will help you realize the extent to which, regardless of budget, you can produce a high-quality music video with a high-production value. You will discover more than the techniques involved—you will understand the strategy behind those techniques. You will not only become a better prepared creative director of your project, but also a savvier marketer—one who knows old school as well as the latest, cutting edge new school techniques for presenting yourself in the best possible way.

You will also find out how you can let the world know about your music video through the Internet. So, how does one approach the topic of making a music video and putting it on the Internet? If you think about it, there are really three main components of this endeavor: the music, the video, and the Internet.

Although they can be thought of independently—and in fact in many circumstances, they are completely independent of each other—you will find that the interrelatedness of these three pieces is the key to making a *good* music video and posting it on the Internet. As such, the book is organized into three easy parts—Part I, The Music; Part II, The Video; and Part III, The Internet.

Part I

Creating Your Music

So, how do you approach the topic of making a music video and posting it on the Internet? If you think about it, there are really three main components of this endeavor: the music, the video, and the Internet.

Although they can be thought of independently, and in fact, in many circumstances they are completely independent of each other, you will find that the interrelatedness of these three pieces is the key to making a *good* music video and posting it on the Internet. As such, the book is organized into three easy pieces: The Music, The Video, and The Internet.

Let's start with the first piece—the music. No matter what kind of music video you plan to make, you should first ensure that the music is strong enough to stand on its own. Although you wouldn't expect to have a compelling experience by watching a video with the audio turned off, you *would* expect that listening to the music without seeing the video would result in a satisfying experience. As a matter of fact, there are certainly times when people have music videos playing on the television in the background while they do something else, unable to see the television screen at all. If it were your music video playing, wouldn't you want it to be a pleasant experience for the listener, in and of itself?

So before you go too far down the road on your particular project, focus on the key piece—the numero uno consideration—the *pièce de résistance*—the music.

The Process

T HE PROCESS OF WORKING ON the music for your music video may vary, depending on whether you want to use an existing track of music or record a new piece specifically for the video. And note that I'm talking about *your* music—original music—a song or instrumental that you or someone in your band has created. If you are planning to make a music video out of someone else's work, it might be a useful exercise or practice session for the real deal. But you won't be able to post it. You won't be able to air it—unless, of course, you're planning on being sued (or you get written permission from the artist). Enough said.

In almost all cases, the music is the roadmap for the visual. You are likely going to illustrate whatever the music (and more than likely, I'm talking about *lyrics* here) is doing at any given point. This does not mean you are confined to producing a literal translation of your lyrics into videotape. You can, after all, use abstract imagery or special effects to get the right mood across in certain cases. Still, it is the music that is driving everything else, including instrumental music that doesn't include lyrics. At the very least, the music video should evoke a mood or emotions—reactions that are strong enough to make the viewers remember the song and/or the artist. The music is the master of the project.

As you can imagine, all of these considerations will involve some thinking and some planning. As a general rule, you wouldn't grab one of your songs, go outside with a video camera, and shoot an entire music video from scratch. And yes, although rules are meant to be broken (by those who understand them), I wouldn't recommend the unplanned, random, stream-of-consciousness approach. (The exception to this rule applies to millionaires who have lots of free time.)

If you're going to use an existing track for your music video, you may want to skip ahead to Chapter 2, "Mixing Considerations". And if you are planning to record a new track, the following sections may prove to be useful to you.

Recording a New Track

How will you go about recording a new track? Assuming you've got the right kind of song in mind, you still have choices about the recording process itself. You may choose to use one of the following:

> ▷ Digital Audio Workstation, or DAW

> ▷ Multitrack recorder, either analog or digital

> ▷ A professional recording studio

All of these are viable choices, and the one you use depends on your particular situation.

Using a DAW

Because it's 2010, most people who use the DIY (do-it-yourself) method will likely opt to use a Digital Audio Workstation (DAW). (I *could* say DIY with a DAW, but I won't.) This is because of several reasons; among them are that the majority of songwriters, composers, and music hobbyists have DAWs in their own homes or project studios. Another very good reason is that this particular group of people might also have desktop video software, which would make the whole prospect of creating a music video very compelling; all of it could be accomplished using a single desktop computer. Today's desktop audio systems have reduced an entire room of recording equipment to a sleek desktop system, as shown in Figures 1.1 and 1.2.

Figure 1.1
An "old" 1990s project studio would easily fill up a room with recording equipment.

Figure 1.2
Today's typical DAW (Digital Audio Workstation) reduces an entire studio to a compact desktop system.

Stop for a second and give notice to this amazing fact. You can make a complete music video, at home, using a sequencer and desktop video software. You can then make multiple DVDs to distribute or video files to post on the Internet. All of this can be done with prosumer computer setups that are more powerful than the computers that took us to the moon! This is certainly something worth noting, in a stop-and-smell-the-roses kind of way. Okay, let's move on.

If you choose the DIY method, a DAW makes a lot of sense because you can:

▷ Be in complete control of the music production.

▷ Choose to change the music later on if needed.

▷ Make sure that all of the technical considerations (file types, sync issues, and so on) are handled correctly.

▷ Edit the video yourself and make changes late in the process if desired.

▷ Have greater control even if you choose to use a professional editor.

Having greater control when using outside resources really applies to any and all outside resources you might use. When you have a desktop workstation, especially one equipped with both music sequencing and desktop video software, you can get into the heart of the project during multiple iterations or versions of the music video as it progresses. You can use the desktop software to try things out on your own, or to examine first-hand how the editor pieced together a particular section. If you created the music tracks on your sequencer, you can make extremely precise edits to the music if it should prove necessary. You can experiment with sound effects and video effects without altering the original file—until you're confident that you want to use them.

Using a Multitrack Recorder

A multitrack recorder can mean analog machines, such as those manufactured by Studer or Fostex (see Figure 1.3). A multitrack recorder can also mean digital multitrack recorders such as those from Tascam or Alesis (see Figure 1.4). Although not as commonly used as a DAW, multitracks are still around, and you, in fact, might want to choose this method of recording.

The *good news* is that you can make a music video based on a track or song created with a multitrack recorder.

Figure 1.3
A multitrack analog machine will require razor-blade editing if you need to make changes later.

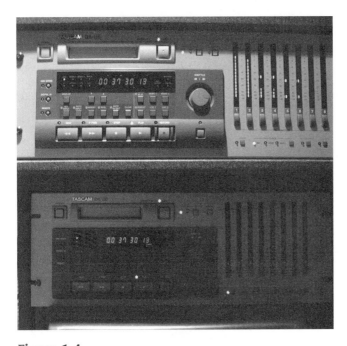

Figure 1.4
A digital multitrack has some benefits over analog, but still does not provide the flexibility of a DAW.

The *bad news* is that some of the key advantages of using a DAW go away. You will have a difficult—sometimes impossible—time trying to make changes to the music later in the process. Random access digital audio and video make this relatively easy. Making changes using linear machines—analog or digital—usually will require redoing tracks that were recorded early on, not to mention re-mixing and re-mastering the final stereo mix. And, if you do make changes that ultimately do not work, you have to go back to the drawing board yet again. All of this can make for a difficult process.

Warning

By far, the biggest disadvantage of not using a DAW is that there is no Undo button! Ouch! Do you remember what life was like before that one little feature shown in Figure 1.5? If you've been using computer-based systems for any amount of time, the ability to undo is second nature. It's expected, commonplace, and matter-of-fact. When you lose that capability, it can be quite a shock, especially when it comes to creating music videos.

Undo

Figure 1.5
The greatest advantage of digital over analog: the Undo option.

A multitrack recorder can be your choice for creating the music for a music video. In reality, it will have to be mixed to a two-track stereo mix, which can be analog linear or random access digital. But to make actual changes (other than removing an entire verse or chorus or intro, and so on) will require you to go back to the original multitrack version, and that's where the difficulties reside. A DAW definitely wins out over the multitrack in most scenarios.

Using a Professional Studio

Perhaps you've already determined that you want to use a professional recording studio to create the music tracks for your video.

There are certainly advantages to using a professional studio when:

▷ You want to record a band or ensemble live and the studio is equipped for it.

▷ The studio has great gear, a good reputation, and an engineer you can work with.

▷ You are using an outside producer and he has an established relationship with the studio.

▷ You have a sizeable budget (or a rich uncle).

Of these possible advantages, the first one is likely the strongest. If you have your own project studio but want to record bass, drums, guitars, keyboards, and vocalists—*live*—then a professional recording studio will provide the right environment for that.

But there might be disadvantages as well (similar to the ones mentioned in the previous multitrack section), if the studio does not use Pro Tools or Logic or some other digital-based, random-access recording method. If the studio is using linear (or even digital) analog machines, you will have a much greater challenge if you need to make changes later. Even at that, changes required after the original mixdown session will require booking more studio time—which is a reminder of another disadvantage: *cost*. It's one thing to work in your own project studio at any time you want, and another to be paying hourly rates as those hours start to accumulate. I know this from experience—both as a buyer of studio time and as a former studio owner.

You would also need to ensure that the studio has some sort of sync-to-video setup, so that whatever changes you are making later in the game are guaranteed to work. Leaving things up to chance is never a good idea, especially in critical timing situations that are measured in frames or milliseconds.

The advantages of random access digital systems, meaning DAWs, make them clear winners over the old school method of linear recording, whether analog or digital. Think of it this way: Would you prefer to use a word processer or a typewriter to create a document? The differences are that dramatic.

Recording Live versus Overdubbing

First, consider the number of tracks you want to end up with. If you were to take that statement literally, the answer would be two—a stereo mix consisting of a left and a right channel. No matter which method you use to record—analog or digital, DAW or studio—you will ultimately end up with a two-track mix. The process of how you get to that final product may be different.

You may be in a band and so you choose to use a professional studio, enabling you to fit everyone in the room and to record live or simultaneously. You may be a singer/songwriter who plays acoustic guitar—and so you choose to record live to capture the feeling or emotion of a live recording. You can record live to a two-track (that is, stereo) recorder or to a multitrack recorder.

Some artists are *studio artists*—meaning they don't perform well in live situations, but they know how to take advantage of all the tools that a studio has to offer. This artist may choose to lay down individual tracks, one at a time, or in concert with a few other musicians.

The important point to remember is that you are not confined to an either-or situation. Even a live recording can be sweetened, which may mean adding a few extra tracks, or cleaning up the existing tracks, or both. The important point to keep in mind is that the recording you're doing will be the foundation for a music video. For example, if you record your band in order to capture that live feeling and adding strings fits well with your particular song, that's fine. But unless you will be using cutaway shots, make sure your keyboard player—the one who plays the strings on his or her synthesizer—shows up to the video shoot. So the main issue here is not whether you have to choose recording live or overdubbing or both. The main issues are looking ahead at the video shoot, and planning ahead, which will make a huge difference later.

Finding a Studio

If you don't have your own studio, finding a professional one should not be too much of a problem in this day and age. Every major (and minor) city has recording facilities of some sort. What can vary is the *type* of studio. At the high end you will find studios that may have 24-track (or more) capabilities, including a Pro Tools setup, an array of instruments, and a nice lounge that includes a spa. This will be one price. (I don't know whether Conway Studios, shown if Figure 1.6, has a spa or not, but it is one of the best studios in L.A.) Another price may apply to a studio that portrays itself as professional but really exists in the owner's garage and causes you to take breaks every time a jet aircraft flies overhead to land at the nearby airport. You *might* be able to make a decent recording in this studio—in some amount of time. Just make sure that Studio B (the one in the garage) doesn't charge the same prices as Studio A. You have every right to check out the studio beforehand to ensure that it meets your needs.

A professional recording studio can offer a lot of bang for your buck—more gear, higher quality, and a professional engineer. If you have the bucks and can afford it, then a professional studio may be the right choice for you. But remember, the editing flexibility that a DAW offers you is hard to beat, and even pro studios don't have an Undo button for every possible situation.

Photo Courtesy of Conway Studios

Figure 1.6
Conway Studios is one of L.A.'s best studios, offering traditional multitrack recording as well as Pro Tools systems.

Mixing
Considerations

There is a well known book by Stephen Covey called *The Seven Habits of Highly Effective People.* In this book, he describes one of the principles as "Begin with the End in Mind." He means to begin each day, task, or project with a clear vision of your desired destination. This is true in life and is applicable to the topic of this chapter. Before you begin mixing, you should have a clear vision of the end product and anticipate the technical considerations that might apply.

In the prior era of making records (these were actually made of vinyl and played on a device known as a "record player"), you had to take into consideration everything about a mix as it applied to the record and the radio, and very occasionally, the television set. By today's terms, this was fairly straightforward. You might have checked the mix on large speakers, small speakers (usually *Auratones*, which were very small, simple, and unflattering), and in both mono and stereo formats. But that was about it. Those were the good old days.

In the digital era of today, things become a bit more complicated, and in this chapter, I will explore some of those issues. Sure, I'll talk about stereo and mono, but there is also the issue of compression. And compression, it turns out, can mean two entirely different processes: audio compression (also called "brick-wall limiting"), which can be used to make a track sound louder, and file compression, a process that squeezes your file size down until it screams "enough already."

Yes, the digital age is much more technical. You need to understand sample rates, bit depth, codecs, and file formats—some of which apply to audio and others that apply to video. This chapter explores these issues, but you need to keep one thing in mind. No matter how technical or "tweaky" you get with your tracks, always ask yourself if the *music* itself sounds good enough.

Getting the Quality You Want

Question: When is good enough *not* good enough?

Answer: When you're putting your whole reputation and chance for success into a three-minute music video that represents the best possible *you*.

There was a day when the phrase "That's good enough" represented an adequate, acceptable level of professionalism on any given project. That time period ended in the Stone Age with the production of the very last iron spear. Today is another story. Today presents a no holds barred, no excuses, better-be-great-or-you-lose scenario.

There are reasons for this. Among them, you are working in a very, very competitive field. While you read this last sentence, it's quite possible that 14 music videos were completed and posted on the Internet. (Okay, it's *possible*—I didn't say it was an absolute fact.) I may not have the statistics, but it's a well-known fact that people in the creative arts are facing more competition than ever before, including in the fields of music, video, music videos, film, television graphic arts, ballet—you name it.

You, as well as your competitors, have access to technology that allows you to create professional output. It's a "no-excuses" world out there, with lots of people scrambling to make their dreams come true.

If your final product doesn't absolutely floor you—and make you convinced that it cannot be beat—then it's not good enough.

Think of it this way: In the "old days," you could make a demo of a song and use that as your "calling card." A demo implied, "When I get a real studio and a real budget, I can make the real thing." For the most part, people are not making demos anymore—they're making masters.

You can hear talk among musicians and engineers in the studio environment, some of which is relevant to the concept of "good enough." The following table shows just a few examples.

What Common Sayings Really Mean

Saying	Actual Meaning
It's good enough.	It's sub-par, possibly acceptable; let's move on.
It's too good to be true.	It is false.
That's good enough for now.	You'll regret this later.
We'll fix it in the mix.	I'm impatient; thank goodness we're working with digital media.

Turning Up the Music with Compression

One of the technicalities that didn't apply to mixing in "the old days" is the topic of compression. You will see that compression can mean a couple of processes—using compression (or limiting) to increase the perceived loudness of a track, and the other type of compression —using specific algorithms to reduce file size while hopefully maintaining a decent amount of quality. I'd like to address the first type of compression first.

One of the trends in today's music is making the tracks sound as loud as possible. By the use of "maximizers" or "brick-wall limiters" (see Figure 2.1), engineers and musicians work to get the apparent level so high that it seems louder than any other track out there. Indeed, it may "sound louder," but at what price? The price can be the loss of dynamic range. Because the lower-level audio is maximized to sound louder, the louder sections cannot exceed a certain threshold without distorting. (For argument's sake, say 0 dB.) So, if done properly, the audio hits a ceiling that may not contain distortion; however, the overall sound seems "squashed." The apparent difference between the lower-level sounds and the louder ones is reduced to the point where dynamic range is severely compromised.

The sad truth, however, is that almost everyone is using this mastering technique to keep up with the rat race for producing louder tracks. So what do you do? The best answer is to find a compromise—a middle-of-the-road that doesn't squash the track too much but is boosted enough to sound loud, even if not as loud as the loudest tracks out there.

Figure 2.1
The L-1 Ultramaximizer from Waves was one of the first maximizer plug-ins.

This may take some experimentation, but the results can be worth it. And because I'm talking about music videos here, getting the right balance is critical so that you sound, at a minimum, competitive. I will caution, however, that if your music is orchestral in nature, it is best to give it the most natural dynamic range possible, with only the loudest peaks hitting the highest threshold before distortion. Nothing sounds worse than strings and horns squashed to only one level with no variations in dynamics.

Mixing for Stereo and Mono

Although brick-wall limiting may not have been a consideration in the making of records, the issues of mixing for stereo and mono in the digital age can sometimes apply. In "ancient" times, when studios were producing records for radio or music videos for television, the topic of creating a stereo mix along with a mono-compatible mix came up often. You didn't know if your music would be heard on an old record player, CD player, or television set that didn't have stereo sound (although, admittedly, it would have been difficult to find CDs that were being played on mono systems). So, because of issues like phasing—or the stereo channels getting out of phase—many steps were taken to ensure that the final stereo mix sounded good on a mono system. Some simply played the stereo mix on a mono system to check it out, while others used mixing boards that had a "mono switch," allowing them to hear a sum of the left and right channels to ensure that the audio was up to par.

While you might choose to take these extra steps, it is fairly unlikely that you would have to. If your music video is going to be posted on the Internet, the playback systems are likely to be PC speakers hooked up to the computer's audio output, which is stereo. If it is played on a Mac, it has stereo audio outputs as well as internal stereo speakers. The plain fact is that for the most part, mono has gone the way of a dinosaur. If you are going to spend extra work cycles on your final mix, focus your energy on something else, such as sample rates and file formats.

Understanding Sample Rates and Bit Depth

A wide variety of sample rates are used in today's audio recordings, and it can sometimes be confusing to know which ones to use (let alone understand what sample rates actually mean). Briefly, a sample rate refers to the number of "snapshots" that are taken of an audio signal every second. Higher sample rates provide more detail in an audio signal. Common sample rates are 44.1 kHz, popularized by the compact disc, and 48 kHz, popularized by the DAT (digital audio recorder). In recent years, higher sample rates such as 96 kHz and 192 kHz have entered the picture, spurred on by the advent of the audio DVD and the never-ending quest to have higher quality sound. Most modern interfaces that convert audio from the analog world into a computer use a variety of sample rates, including some of the higher ones.

Another aspect of sound quality is determined by *bit depth*. Higher bit depths yield higher audio resolution in terms of dynamic range. Low-quality audio, such as appeared in the first computer games on the PC, usually had a bit depth of eight bits. CD audio is 16-bit. And like the higher sampling rates that provide high-quality audio, higher bit rates contribute to better audio and have appeared in the form of 24-bit resolution. That's why you may see audio specs today that advertise 96 kHz/24-bit resolution and other high-end sample rates and bit depths.

When all is said and done, however, CDs can play back only in 44.1 kHz/16-bit resolution, and the audio tracks for video play back at 48 kHz/16-bit. So why all the fuss about using higher rates for recording if it's going to be down-sampled when you're done? The reasoning is that using higher sample and bit rates will yield a better audio recording, even if it has to be down-sampled at the end of the process.

What you decide to use in your recording is ultimately up to you. You might try auditioning DVD audio discs and other audio programs that play back at higher rates to see if you can hear the difference. Some people swear by it, meaning they can hear much better quality in these formats. Others attest that there is no audible difference.

The bottom line is that you should never go below the lowest and most common spec for video, which is 48 kHz/16-bit.

Coming to Terms with Codecs and File Formats

Never before in the history of mankind has there been anything so gloriously confusing as audio and video file formats, bit depths, and compression algorithms. Okay, maybe there are things more confusing somewhere (such as the credit crisis that began in the fall of 2008, for example). But, for certain, these bits of technology are in the top ten. To make things even more interesting, there are codecs, file types, and container formats—some of which are used interchangeably or simultaneously to mean the same thing, or even different things. Confused yet?

You don't need to become an expert in these topics—unless you want to, of course—but you do need to have enough of an understanding to make the right choices at the right time for your audio and video production needs. I hope the following discussion will give you enough ammunition to put up a good fight in the format jungle.

Understanding Codecs

What, you might ask, is a codec, and what's its purpose? First, I discuss its purpose. Because of the large size of audio and video files, compression is necessary, and you reduce their size by use of a codec. The compression side or coding aspect of the term is the *co* of codec, whereas the decompression or decoding side of the process is the *dec*. Put them together and you have a *codec*. Using compression, by means of a codec, you make video manageable in terms of its file size. This process also optimizes a file's bandwidth so that it can be streamed efficiently over the Internet.

A variety of codecs have certain advantages or disadvantages for audio and video files, depending on the specific applications of the digital media file. There are also two major categories of codec—lossy and lossless.

Lossy codecs reduce the actual size of the data in order to achieve compression while utilizing specific algorithms to give the *impression* that all of the data is there. To put it another way, a lossy codec shrinks the file size in a sneaky way so that no one (hopefully) will notice it.

A *lossless* codec compresses a file without discarding any data. The choice of what codec to use in a given situation usually depends on whether a small file size is of great importance (in which case, a lossy codec is used) or whether quality is of paramount importance (in which case, a lossless codec is the better choice).

One source of confusion when attempting to understand codecs is that some of them are actually a specific type of algorithm for compressing/decompressing a file and some are file format. To make life more interesting, some of them are *both*.

Codecs are discussed in more detail in Chapter 10, "Making Your Video Internet-Ready," especially as they apply to putting your video online.

Using compression accomplishes two main goals: It reduces the file size of the video and compresses it for smooth streaming on the Internet. Both of these tasks are necessary for the production of music videos for the Internet.

Understanding Audio Formats

The multitude of file formats available for audio has been the result of many years of competition between different computer platforms (Apple and Microsoft come to mind), as well as surprising yet effective innovations, such as the ubiquitous MP3 format.

If I were to discuss every single file format that has emerged in the last decade due to the transition to digital media, I would have to write a separate book on the topic (and frankly, I'd rather not). So, I'll keep the discussion focused on the file formats that relate to the making of music videos.

Here are the most common audio file formats that are of interest to you:

> ▷ **AAC—Advanced Audio Coding:** Audio format popularized by Apple's iTunes that uses sophisticated compression algorithms designed to improve the MP3 format. Files usually have an extension of .mp4 (because it is a version of the MPEG-4 standard).

> ▷ **AIFF—Audio Interchange File Format:** Common audio format for both Mac and Windows, although it is much more common on the Mac.

- ▷ **AU—Audio Units:** A system-level architecture for audio plug-ins used by Apple's Core Audio in the Mac operating system.

- ▷ **WAV:** The original audio file format from Microsoft.

- ▷ **MP3—MPEG-1, Audio Level 3:** A popular audio file format that uses a great deal of compression to make files roughly one-tenth of their original size. MP3 uses effective compression algorithms that eliminate or reduce sound outside the range of human hearing.

- ▷ **WMA—Windows Media Audio:** An audio codec and file format from Microsoft that is their answer to MP3.

Understanding Video Formats

The variety of video formats has also been the result of computer platform wars. Added to that, several innovations have come from the video and film industries. Listed here are the most common and relevant to the process of making music videos:

- ▷ **AVI—Audio/Video Interleaved:** One of the first video file formats. It was developed by Microsoft.

- ▷ **DivX:** A video codec often used for downloading video from the Internet. It is based on MPEG-4 and uses AVI as its container format. (I told you this topic is confusing!)

- ▷ **WMV—Windows Media Video:** Microsoft's current video file format.

- ▷ **QT—QuickTime:** As close to a standard as you can get that works on both the Mac and the Windows operating systems.

- ▷ **MPEG-4:** A container format for audio and video. If both audio and video are present, the filename .mp4 will be present. If it is audio only, the file has an .m4a extension.

- ▷ **H.264:** An advancement of MPEG-4 that provides high-quality video frames up to four times the original size.

As of this writing, H.264 is one of the most popular formats along with Apple's QuickTime. Very often, a QuickTime movie (of which you will be making many) is reduced in size to the H.264 format, which most often uses AAC for the audio portion of your program. During the compression process, you will have options for choosing what kind of file format, file size, screen size, and audio compression method you want to use.

Try to familiarize yourself with the file formats mentioned in this section. However, if you are in a hurry (who isn't?) and want to cut to the chase, the following section can be used as a reliable "one-stop" guideline for which file formats and compression methods to use.

Compression Methods: The Bottom Line

If you study codecs, file formats, container formats, and fractals long enough, rest assured you will get a migraine headache. So, to simplify this topic, here are some helpful hints about compressing video:

▷ **Watch and rewatch your video before compressing it.** The compression process can take a long time and the last thing you want is to find a couple of small errors in the original video that require you to start over. Watch, rewatch, compress.

▷ **Use QuickTime to compress your video.** More specifically, use QuickTime Pro, which is the professional version that contains all of the tools you need for compression and is available for both the Mac operating system and for Windows. If you already have the regular version of QuickTime, you already have QuickTime Pro, because when you purchase the Pro version, you're given a code that unlocks it.

▷ **Use H.264 for compression.** Set the data rate somewhere between 500 Kbps (kilobytes per second) and 7500 Kbps, keeping in mind that the larger numbers also mean larger file sizes. With compression comes experimentation—it's the law.

▷ **If your aspect ratio is standard (4 × 3), then your screen dimensions should be 640 × 480 (or an exact equivalent of that).** If your aspect ratio is widescreen at 16 × 9, then choose 720 by a number from 405 to 480 (experiment with this as your mileage may vary). Finally, if you're working with HD, then you're probably looking at 1280 × 720. Whatever the case, especially with letterbox format, make sure you select Preserve Aspect Ratio using either letterbox or crop.

▷ **Make sure you select Optimize for Streaming.** This is important for posting video on the Internet. With this setting, viewers can start watching the video while it's still downloading.

▷ **For audio, use the AAC codec.** Set the bit rate no lower than 128 Kbps and ideally 160 or 192 Kbps.

Compression can be a daunting task, even for professionals in the business. But it is a critical process that can help to ensure that your video looks and sounds its best. When it comes to music videos, that's very, very important.

See Chapter 10 for additional details on compression and file formats that are used to make your music video Internet-ready.

Part II

Producing Your Video

Music Video Cookbook:

The Ingredients

MOST GOOD COOKS HAVE HAD some training, perhaps from a culinary school in New York or Paris. Sure, there are exceptions, such as the talented people who can put together an incredible meal without using as much as a measuring cup, let alone a recipe book. But for the most part, being armed with knowledge is a good thing, especially if you don't have a lot of experience yet. Creating a music video by understanding the elements that go into it can result in a tasty audio-visual treat, and that includes studying many of the music videos that already exist.

Songs and Tracks
that Make Good Videos

As I mention in Chapter 1, "The Process," one important point you will need to determine is whether to use an existing song as the basis for your music video or record a new one.

But before you decide whether to use an existing track or record a new one, ask yourself if the song you have in mind is the best candidate for a music video. Here are some of the things to consider:

> ▷ It's not the genre of music that counts (such as rock, pop, country, and so on); rather, it's whether the music and lyrics can be a foundation for creating visual imagery to go with the song.

> ▷ It doesn't matter whether you think the song is a "single" or an album cut. (Are there really such things as singles and albums anymore?) What matters is that it's good music that stands on its own merits and works well with video.

> ▷ Whatever song you have in mind must be capable of sparking ideas for the video. If it's a real stretch to think that the track will work as a music video, it's not the right song. Will it tell a story? Or will it evoke emotional reactions? If it does neither, you may be picking the wrong track.

> ▷ The song you use should be three or four minutes long. If it's any longer, you are going to have a difficult time keeping your attention deficit disordered viewers dialed in (not to mention the viewers who *don't* have ADD).

Story, Emotion, and Imagination

Not every song tells the most powerful story ever imagined. But, just as in films, a strong story moves things along and gives viewers a sense of satisfaction. Does that mean a music video can't consist of a cool track and a bunch of visual effects? Well, if you were to ask Roland Emmerich, the man behind *Independence Day, The Day After Tomorrow*, and *2012*, he would probably be a strong advocate of a special effects-based experience. But with heavy visual effects come much higher budgets, something for you to keep in mind.

The story is your plot. The story is the essence of your song. The story is the inspiration for your music video.

The Value of Story

One thing I've learned from experience is that all the special effects in the world cannot help a visual experience unless it is built upon a strong story. The teachers of this fact have been Steven Spielberg, George Lucas, James Cameron, and many other filmmakers—both good and bad. You may know the feeling of leaving a theater feeling empty, in spite of the fact that there were a great deal of explosions, car chases, and CGI (computer-generated images) creatures to last anyone for a lifetime. What is sometimes missing is a *story*—a narrative—something that draws you into the plot. Beyond that is the need for character development—do you have a sense of who the characters are, what makes them tick, and what motives are driving them to do what they do? Do you *care* about them?

A filmmaker should be able to tell a good story in a timeframe of two hours or more. You might argue that a short-form music video is a different animal and that telling a story in three or four minutes is a lot more difficult. And you would be right—it is more difficult. But is it necessary?

The answer is yes—and no. Many music videos are story-driven. The lyrics of the song provide the roadmap for the visuals. In most of these cases, the original song and its lyrics *are* the story. The visuals illustrate this story. The illustration can be literal or figurative, or both. But combined, the music, lyrics, and video work together to convey a story, an idea, and a three-minute vignette on some aspect of life.

If your music video does not communicate a story, at the very least, it should stir *emotion*.

The Value of Emotion

Try watching a video sometime without the soundtrack. Suppose, for argument's sake, that you could still hear the dialogue but not the music. You will likely find that the film drags and drags and drags along. You might find that you lose interest in the plot and the characters. Even if you don't, you may discover that the movie leaves you flat. You understand what it is trying to communicate, but you don't feel *moved* by it.

A music video, whether story-driven or not, should evoke some sort of emotion from your audience. There may be an overarching emotion that you want to communicate, and the video may have more than one emotion contained within it. A video that doesn't rely on story may instead be based on a *situation*. Still, a situational piece will convey certain emotions—fear, love, hate, suspense, regret, elation, and of course the list goes on. If your song is constructed in such a way that the emotional content is obvious, then congratulations —your job is somewhat easier. But if what the video is trying to communicate is not obvious, lyrically, you will need to dig deeper and ask yourself some questions that will lead you to the emotional context of your piece. As is the case with the need for story, the need for emotion is vital. Is it absolutely necessary? Perhaps not. But at the very least, your video should stir the *imagination*.

The Value of Imagination

If you haven't already seen it, rent and enjoy *2001: A Space Odyssey* (It's available on Netflix, as seen in Figure 3.1). Although it *does* have a story and it *does* convey emotion, the strongest suit of this film is the way it stirs the imagination. When it was first released, nothing like it had ever been seen. Much of the story must be filled in by your imagination and is subject to your own interpretation. The emotional context can also vary widely based upon your particular interpretation. There is a part in the film that relies on visual effects that, when compared to those of today, are somewhat primitive but that still stir your imagination—immensely. The motion picture relies heavily on the viewer's imagination in order to make it a satisfying movie experience.

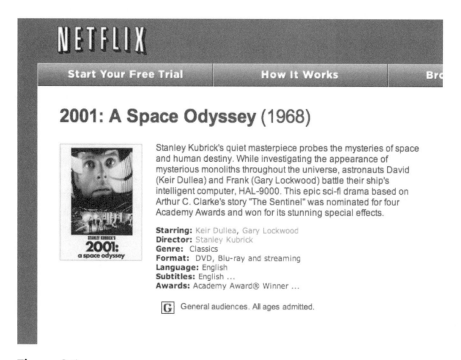

Figure 3.1
2001: A Space Odyssey was a game-changing film in 1968 that is available for rent and is guaranteed to stir your imagination.

Stirring the imagination can also be the primary goal of a music video. While a story-driven video will lean toward a literal representation of the music, an imagination-driven video will be primarily a figurative, abstract representation of an idea. Naturally, these lines can be blurred, in that some videos have content that falls into both of these categories.

If imagination turns out to be your primary vehicle or goal, make sure that it's not so abstract that viewers will be scratching their heads, wondering what they just saw. There needs to be an even balance of abstract ideas on one hand and easy-to-understand concepts on the other to achieve a satisfying viewing experience. Again, *2001: A Space Odyssey* serves as an excellent example of this balance.

Your Homework Assignment: Watch TV, Visit the Web

Bet you never got this homework assignment in school, did you?

All kidding aside, it would be a very good exercise to study what kinds of music videos are already on the web or on television. Instead of zoning out, however, you need to pay close attention to what you're seeing and hearing. Take notes. Write down which videos grab and keep your attention—including where you saw them. If you have a DVR (digital video recorder), you can tape hours of them if you want—and watch them when you can.

When you go on the web, do the same thing—pay attention and take notes. Bookmark the web pages that have videos you like. You might even bookmark the pages that you don't like so that you'll know what not to do later.

For the time being, don't get stuck on quality issues, such as how good the videos look on your widescreen, HD television, compared to the much smaller, low-res images on the web. As you will see later in Chapter 10, "Making Your Video Internet-Ready," to get video files small enough to fit on the web, you have to use compression —and that affects the picture quality. Keep in mind, however, that most of those videos start out in a much better resolution. The compression of the video file is applied much later and after the fact. Concentrate on content, more than anything else.

Learning from Others

There are lots of "old sayings" I could write here, such as "Those who do not learn from history are bound to repeat it," and many others along that line. But if I did, I would sound preachy, and I don't want to go down that path. The study of music videos is not like the study of history, however, and that might make you a little more eager to take a look at some of the music videos that are on television and the Internet.

Music Videos on Television

After watching a lot of music videos on television, be careful not to copy something directly from someone else. Your goal should be to grasp the ideas and the general concepts behind the videos. As the saying goes, "Don't reinvent the wheel." By watching music videos—lots of music videos—you can discover what spokes make up the music video wheel.

Once you start watching music videos, it doesn't take long to realize how different they can be from one another. When you think of a music video, the tendency may be to think in terms of how music videos were constructed when they first appeared on channels such as MTV or VH1. The common formula was to show different camera angles of the artist or band while it lip synced to the song. There may have been a few cut-aways and some sort of video special effects here and there. The title of the song, artist, and record label appeared in the lower-left corner at the beginning of the song and sometimes at the end as well. And that was it—that's what comprised a music video.

While you may still find music videos that fit this particular formula, they have come a long way since then and now have a variety of forms. This topic is covered in more detail in Chapters 6, "Choosing a Video Style," and 7, "Shooting Options," but suffice it to say that there is no singular formula for a successful music video. You can find a good example of a video that breaks the mold with "Here It Goes Again" by OK Go. Check it out on YouTube at www.youtube.com. (Type **here it goes again** into the Search box.)

Music Videos on the Internet

Because people are no longer limited to television as their single source of entertainment, and because the subject at hand involves posting music videos on the Internet, it makes a lot of sense to watch some of the music videos you can find online. What's that? You say you can't afford to sign up for a music video service? No problemo.

There are tons of videos you can watch for free at sites such as these:

new.music.yahoo.com

music.aol.com

rhapsody.com

myspace.com

vh1.com

mtv.com/music

If you want to find more sites, use a search engine such as Google and enter the phrase: **music videos online free**. That will keep you busy for hours on end. Some sites will keep videos rotating automatically, just in case you're tired of clicking the mouse button.

Make sure you make *variety* a goal when you are searching through music videos. It is very easy to pick your favorite genre, such as the one in which your particular music fits, at the expense of missing out on other forms of music videos that might inspire your creativity. Remember, this is homework, and you are studying for your exam. Your exam is the video you will be producing, so do your research now while you can. Expose yourself to as much variety as possible because this is where you will get ideas and inspiration, regardless of your particular genre of music.

Music Videos of the Homegrown Variety

Don't forget that there are thousands of never-seen-before music videos that are not on the "mainstream" channels. So part of your homework assignment should be to check out what music videos other people—many of them in a similar situation such as you—have posted on sites such as Vimeo.com (see Figure 3.2), veoh.com, and many others. (See Chapter 11, "Evaluating Popular Online Sites," for more of these sites.) You can even include sites such as youtube.com that, although they aren't singularly devoted to music videos, still have many music videos that are more of the homegrown variety.

Figure 3.2
Vimeo is one of many sites you can use for uploading your music videos. Check it out at vimeo.com.

In fact, some of the lines get blurred when you look at a site such as myspace.com. Are the videos on myspace.com coming from professionals, aspiring artists, or complete newcomers? The answer is, all of the above. The lines that have historically divided music artists into "signed" and "unsigned" are not as relevant as they used to be. The record industry as a whole—meaning the major labels—is still undergoing dramatic changes.

The good news about these changes is that newcomers have more vehicles for exposure than ever before. So, when you do your homework assignment, don't just look at higher budget, "professional" music videos. There is plenty to learn from those who produce no-budget or low-budget music videos, yet have found creative means to compete at a higher level.

Choosing Your

Production Methods

I F YOU DID THE HOMEWORK assignment in Chapter 3, "Music Video Cookbook: The Ingredients," and watched enough music videos to blur your vision, then it's probably time to get started on *your* music video, right? Wrong. Before you go down the path of producing a music video, you need to determine what *type* of production it's going to be. There are choices to be made that are somewhat determined by budget (actually, determined *a lot* by budget), by the level of professionalism you are looking to achieve, and by the amount of direct control you want to have over the video production process. Each of these choices poses advantages and disadvantages, so if you haven't done so already, take the time to determine which production method will fit your particular music video goals. Also keep in mind that there is an additional choice that involves combining some of these suggested methods to complete your music video on time and on budget.

Method 1—Do It Yourself (DIY)

By far, the biggest motivation for doing it yourself is budget. After all, if you had unlimited funds, wouldn't you hire the best professionals you could find to make your music video? (The correct answer is "yes," in case you didn't know.) But doing it yourself does not necessarily mean that you are making an amateur video. Remember, as I mentioned earlier in this book, you are the *prosumer*, and you can consider the "pro" part of prosumer to mean *professional results* instead of a previous definition of "pro" as meaning the *producer*.

Dollars and Sense

Let's face it—doing it yourself is going to be the cheapest way to go (although in these circles, it's better to say "lower budget" and to avoid using the word "cheap"). Now, this assumes that you have all or most of the hardware and software you will need for production. If you need to equip a full music and video production project studio, even in a bedroom in your house, and you are starting with nothing, then your startup costs will be quite different. But, as stated earlier in the book, I'm assuming you already have a head start on all of this.

So, back to the budget. Providing you have the basics, there will still be some additional expenses, which may include costs for the following items (some of which are shown in Figure 4.1).

For equipment and accessories, you may need the following:

▷ Storage—MiniDV tapes, extra hard drives, and so on

▷ Lighting, reflectors—If you decide you need a more professional look indoors

▷ Lenses and filters—Not an absolute necessity, but nice to have around

▷ Extra power in the form of batteries

▷ Cables and adaptors—For audio, video, and electric (see Figure 4.2)

For the cast, you may need these items:

▷ Wardrobe

▷ Make-up

▷ Food or catering

▷ Salary (didn't anyone mention that possibility?)

Figure 4.1
Among the items you'll need to consider in your budget are extras like tapes (or other storage) and batteries.

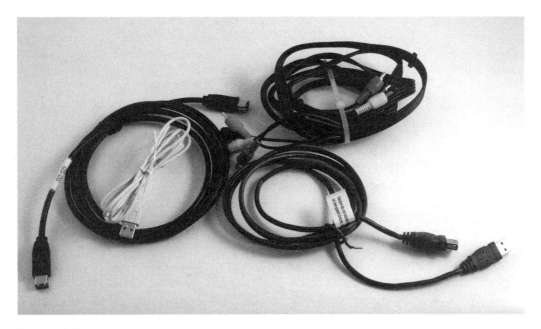

Figure 4.2
You'll need extra cables such as the ones pictured: FireWire, USB, A/V cables (RCA), and more.

For the crew you may need these amenities:

    ▷ Food or catering

    ▷ Salary (didn't anyone mention that possibility?)

Didn't anyone mention salary? Okay, for the sake of argument, let's assume that everyone is going to pitch in for free. This will be a major variable based upon the type of production you're doing, the level of experience of the people involved, and obvious issues, such as whether everyone involved is an integral part of the project—the band, the manager, the roadies, and so on.

In a do-it-yourself project, many of these items will be up to your sole discretion. Of the categories just mentioned, the first one—equipment and accessories—may have items that are unavoidable, such as batteries, cables, and so on. The other categories may either be completely unnecessary or an absolute requirement, such as wardrobe. These items will be determined by your script and whether you need any wardrobe changes or additional crew members.

A Production Toolbox Is Now Available

There was a time that the idea of self-producing a music video with professional-looking (and sounding) results was impossible. That was before we had the tools that are available to us today. It may sound like a cliché, but you have more computer power on your desktop than the astronauts had available to them on their moon landing (and all you're doing is making a music video—you're not even attempting to get into orbit). Moreover, laptop computers have become so powerful that they provide you with the capability to take your production on the road (see Figure 4.3).

The tools, in the form of hardware and software, clearly create an advantage for the do-it-yourselfer of today and more than that, make it even possible. See Chapter 5, "Tools for Do-It-Yourselfers," for a more in-depth look at audio and video production tools.

Control Geeks

Maybe you're not a control freak, but if you're technically and creatively savvy, you can be a control geek. (Combine these with ambition, and you could be the guy in Figure 4.4.) A clear advantage in doing it yourself is that you will have more control. At the very least, you are the director and in some cases, the producer, the writer, the camera operator, the editor, and so on. Sure, you might have friends or colleagues who take on some of these tasks. But when you're in charge, you're in control. So add another advantage to the DIY (do it yourself) column.

Figure 4.3
Now the computer power on your desktop is accessible anywhere you go.

Figure 4.4
Conductors are the type of control freak
that you might not mind having as a friend.

An argument can be made that if you're doing an expensive professional production, you might be in control as well. True, but if you are sharing the expense with others in a team environment (say, members of a band), then you will have more chefs in the kitchen, chefs that are much more vocal because they have dollars at stake.

DIY Can Expand Your Creative and Technical Abilities

There's nothing like on-the-job training, and making a music video will give you plenty of it. When you think about the disciplines involved—audio recording and video production to name a couple—you are only scratching the surface of music video production. There is also the writing, the casting, wardrobe, and many other tasks that will challenge your creativity and technical chops.

If you're an accomplished music video director/producer, then you already know these things, mostly from experience. But if you're just starting out, you will need to "push the envelope" and work on tasks you may never have attempted previously. In addition to books, such as this one, you will benefit by reading about other parts of the process in more specialized areas. For example, what do you know about make-up? Special effects? Camera moves? In addition to this type of self-education, there is the prospect of doing a lot of research on the Internet—before you begin your production, as well as during it, to get information that is very up-to-date. Even if your first project does not meet your expectations, you will have gained valuable experience you can use on your second production. Hiring a professional crew is certainly great, but it won't give you as much direct, hands-on experience as a DIY production does.

Bragging Rights and Building a Reel

After you've got at least one music video project under your belt, you can honestly say that you're a music video director and/or producer. You can add it to your resume, put in on your business card, and introduce yourself that way at cocktail parties. I would not recommend doing so until you have a production that you think is very deserving of the director or producer title. But, at some point in your career (even if it's not your life-long goal to direct music videos), you will be able to tout your music video production capabilities.

A DIY production becomes more than an item on your resume when you realize that what you are really creating is a *reel.* A reel these days means a digital file rather than a physical reel that spins around and around (see Figure 4.5). But then again, many refer to their latest CD as their new *record*, a term that at one time meant something vinyl that also spun around and around. Nevertheless, the clips that you continue to build up in time will become part of your reel or portfolio or demo—whatever name you want to call it.

Additionally, because you are thinking about posting it on the Internet, you will automatically have a promotional and marketing tool you can use to your heart's content.

QuickTime

Figure 4.5
A reel, by any name, is a reel.

Method 2—The Student Filmmaker

As mentioned earlier, there are advantages and disadvantages in each method of production, and using a student filmmaker is no exception. And just like before with the terms "reel" and "record," the term *filmmaker* may be a bit of a misnomer. In most cases, I am really talking about *video*, which ironically enough, is sometimes used to make professional films. Nevertheless, I will stick with the term student filmmaker or film student—as this is the term used in most colleges and film schools.

Two Steps Ahead of You

The clear advantage of teaming up with student filmmakers is that they already have some training and experience, not to mention the confidence that comes with having that experience. They are likely two steps ahead of you, assuming that you've concentrated most of your efforts on songwriting. The film student already knows about camera moves, lighting, file formats, aspect ratios, and post-production—things that you may know *something* about but not enough to call yourself *experienced*. Teaming up with a student filmmaker might yield more professional results and, at the very least, save you a lot of time in every aspect of the production.

Why would a film student want to work with you in the first place? Well, he or she may not. This part of the formula relies on the strength of your act, persuasive capabilities, as well as your ability to network. Getting in touch with film schools and posting your project may be one way to find a student filmmaker. Another is to use the Internet to post an ad for a student filmmaker on websites such as www.craigslist.com or www.mandy.com. You could offer the film student some amount of composing for his productions as a trade for his services. And remember that you can also sweeten your offer with *some* amount of cash, even in a low-budget production.

Gimme Some Gear

A natural built-in advantage to teaming up with a film student is access to equipment that you don't have to buy or rent. The filmmaker may not have a full audio production studio, but hopefully *you* do. Where the student filmmaker comes in is on the video side of things, and she may come not only with a camera, but also with lighting, reflectors, additional lenses, and so on. But it doesn't stop there. If the student filmmaker wants a lot of involvement in the project, you can enlist her to participate in everything from pre-production to final product. Your particular needs may vary as much as the student filmmaker's capabilities do, so approach this method with some flexibility.

Sounding Board

One problem with the DIY method is that you often work alone and may not have anyone to bounce your ideas off of—a sounding board of sorts. With a film student, you automatically have a sounding board with whom you can bounce, debate, discuss, and challenge ideas. This is not to say you won't have this advantage in other methods, except that the DIY method may not present as much opportunity to do so.

Just as in the case of watching other types of music videos outside of your particular genre, working closely with someone like a student filmmaker can help you "think outside the box" and reveal ideas you would not ordinarily think of.

Gather the Crew

Sometimes a student filmmaker comes with other student filmmakers. If there is enough interest in your project, it's not out of the realm of possibility to enlist other film students in executing many of the tasks from pre- to post-production. You could potentially have more than one student to help you—you could have a crew, again, depending on your persuasive abilities and the quality of your music. You might even have a scenario in which you hand off the directing chores to student filmmaker number one while you take on the role of executive producer. It feels good, doesn't it? Don't rule it out.

Built-In Networking

Film students may have a number of connections that can be beneficial to you. It may be that they know someone in the business. Or maybe they know someone who knows some-one. Although it is totally possible that they know no one at all (of any consequence), at the very least, you have networking potential here that you may not have in the DIY scenario.

Many composers today are working with filmmakers whom they either knew from film school or worked with early on. Those relationships are important. If you think you may be doing more music videos in the future, these relationships should be nurtured. When you look at feature films, as an example, you'll notice that directors seem to work with some of the people—especially composers—time after time. If there seems to be synergy between you and the student filmmaker, think in terms that are beyond the scope of this particular music video. You could, in fact, be working in a professional situation with this person years from now, and during those years, the connections that you have will continue to grow.

As always, use the Internet as a resource, too. Just by Googling "student filmmaker," I came across a great site called www.studentfilmmakers.com, which can be a great jumping off point for increasing the size and reach of your network.

Method 3—Professional Video Director

Now you transcend from low/no-budget projects into the "how much is that going to cost?" territory. If your budget and inclination allows for it, using a pro might be the way to go. As with the first two scenarios, this choice poses advantages and disadvantages.

Getting Pro Results

Based on your budget, you may be able to hire a professional to help you with your music video. Also based on your budget, you might be hiring one videographer or a production company that has a full staff of professionals. For the sake of clarity, I'll use the word "professional" to mean either one, unless otherwise specified.

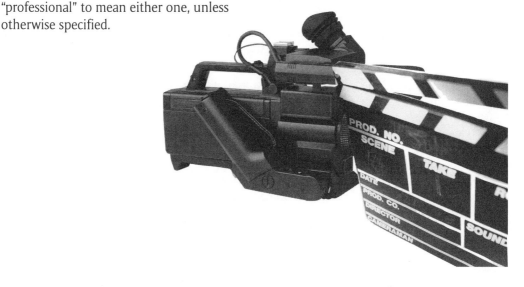

One assumption you can probably make is that hiring a professional will yield professional results—more professional than the other alternatives. In most respects this is true, but there are other things to consider that go beyond the word professional.

▷ **Communication:** When you first interview a professional, get a real sense of how your communication is flowing. If it seems at all awkward, this professional may not be a good fit for you. No matter how much talent the professional might have, if you don't have excellent communication, nothing else will be successful.

▷ **Synergy:** Make sure you are "on the same page" or on the same "wavelength." Although this has a lot to do with communication, it goes beyond that to include other issues. Can you work with this person? Does he have an aesthetic view, a sense of humor, and a work ethic similar to yours? If you're not comfortable at the first meeting, it's unlikely that you'll be comfortable later on.

▷ **Musical aptitude:** Melody, harmony, rhythm—these and many other musical techniques are something you need to know. Of these, if your professional had only a sense of rhythm, your project would benefit greatly. Editing and even camera moves have a sense of rhythm to them. Combine this with the fact that your entire focus is music, so you want the pulse and the heartbeat of your music video as a whole to have good rhythm—which leads to the next point.

▷ **Experience with music videos:** Your professional may have done a ton of corporate videos, television commercials, public service spots, and infomercials, but if music videos are not part of the pro's portfolio, you might be going down the wrong path. This is not to say that it's *impossible* for a pro with another specialty to produce a good music video. But because people do tend to specialize, I would recommend hiring a producer with music video experience, just as I would prefer that a corporate video be produced by a specialist in corporate video, and so on.

▷ **Trust:** All of these considerations, combined, should give a feeling of confidence and trust. This will be very necessary when you begin shooting, for your energies should focus on the creative aspects of the project, not on any of the preceding issues. Although no one producer may be perfect, you are better off not settling for something less than "very good." It is, after all, your budget.

Faster Turn-Around Time

This is a potential advantage when hiring a professional. I say *potential* because although the pro can likely work faster than you on some of these tasks, turn-around time also depends on the current schedule of the pro or production company you're hiring. This is something to talk about directly in your initial meeting. If his or her schedule is full and yours in on a deadline, you don't have a match. If, on the other hand, the pro can get you in on your schedule, the tasks—especially post-production—should go faster and give you a good turn-around time.

Suggestions, Please

Similar to the scenario of the student filmmaker, using an outside resource—in this case, a professional—provides a means of having someone to give you feedback, not only before the shoot, but after it as well. And in this case, your sounding board has a great deal of experience with which to give you ideas, techniques, and who knows—maybe even a connection or two for distribution. Working in isolation can work well, but working as part of a team (providing the synergy is there) can make it even better.

One or More Team Members

You may be hiring one producer/director for your project or a team consisting of writers, cameramen, soundman, film editors, and more. It is likely that you are in the former group (one producer/director) rather than the latter. But if it is a production company—even a small one—ask questions about the structure of their organization and whether other people can be utilized at a reasonable cost. This not only provides faster turn-around time, it gives you the advantage of people who specialize in a particular discipline.

Crossing the Technical Divide

The professional comes with a great deal of technical knowledge, knowledge that you may not have about the variety of formats, file types, and other technical "gotchas." As I point out in the earlier DIY section, these are things you can certainly learn yourself. But if you are more creatively gifted than technically astute, this built-in advantage to using a professional may be your cup of tea.

Choices, Choices

One overarching guideline to choosing your production method is how it will be used. This book focuses on posting your video on the Internet. You may have fantasies about getting it placed on VH1 or MTV as well. If that's the case, the homegrown production may not yield a music video that is broadcast-ready. I say *may* because it certainly is possible to get to this level of professional quality on your own. But in most cases, a goal of a broadcast video would be best served by hiring an outside professional.

Again and again, the issue of *budget* will rear its head. That's because more than any other decision-driver, budget is the master of all. All other considerations aside, if you can't afford to hire a professional, that means some of the points in this chapter are good to know but somewhat inapplicable if you don't have the necessary funds. Yet, sometimes the reverse is true. You may have the budget but a yearning desire to do something on your own—to be your own producer/director, writer, and editor.

The key is to know these things in advance, before you go to the production company for an initial meeting. One of first things they will ask you (instead of telling you how much things cost) is, "What is your budget?" The answer to that will dictate much you can and cannot do.

Tools for

Do-It-Yourselfers

ALONG WITH THE JOY that technology brings to prosumers comes the price tag of confusion. Technology is complex by nature, and although you may know a great deal about each of the three major components of music videos—the music, the video, and the Internet—it is doubtful that you know everything. Even the geekiest of techies does not know everything (although many would like you to think so).

So, starting with the basics, you have to determine what kind of camcorder you will use and what kind of video you will create (HD or standard definition). Assuming you have a computer, you will need to know what editing software to use, and if you don't have a computer, you are standing at the end of the line with thousands of people ahead of you. (However, it's not too late to get a new computer—ever!)

From here, you can acquire whatever complement of tools you feel is necessary, as long as you have the budget for it. For example, you can make a music video with only a camcorder. But you can make a much more impressive video if you have a lighting kit.

Once you have a lighting kit, it makes sense to have extra batteries. While you're at it, you might occasionally need your own power in the form of a generator. If you have all of that, you will discover the need for reflectors, light meters, extra bulbs, and the list goes on. So, although using *just* a camcorder will work, you really have to evaluate—in advance—how sophisticated you want to get. This applies not only to lighting, but also to virtually every aspect of the video-making process: tripods for your camcorder, steadicams, multiple lenses, filters, and so on.

Fortunately, as I discuss later, the cost of the post-production process, especially editing, has come way down due to the advent of sophisticated computer editing programs such as Final Cut Pro, Final Cut Express, Adobe Premiere, Avid Express, and many other brands. This is a relatively new phenomenon, because it wasn't very long ago that these types of nonlinear editing systems were nonexistent. The power of nonlinear editing debuted in early products from Adobe and Avid, and some of the first visual effects were part of the Video Toaster software that ran on the Commodore Amiga computer. Amazing things have been produced with these systems, but by today's standards, those products seem very primitive. The power of professional post-production studios has come down to the home—even to a laptop computer—courtesy of software from companies such as Apple.

Choosing the Right Video Format

First, say goodbye to the analog camcorder and the VHS tape. I'm sure you appreciate all that they've done for you, but there is no better definition of old school than a fifteen-pound camcorder that shoots low-resolution video that plays on a format no one has any more. Enough said.

You need to work with a digital camcorder. This category has a lot of formats to choose from—and no one type fits all. At the end of the twentieth century—around 1998 or 1999—the MiniDV format took over. MiniDV cameras use, not surprisingly, MiniDV tape (see Figure 5.1). The tape is not used at all like analog tape was with VHS systems. The DV tape is recording data—essentially, ones and zeros—of the information from the digital camera. MiniDV can produce near-broadcast–quality video. MiniDV is also the most dominant format today, although there is the "threat" that another format may eventually take over.

Figure 5.1
Many camcorders, such as this Canon, use MiniDV—still the dominant format today.

A more recent format uses a tapeless means of recording data. This may be a hard drive, a CD, a DVD, a memory stick, or some other removable device. Of these, the hard drive seems to be the most popular and may wind up leading the pack. The upside to using MiniDV, however, is that you automatically have a backup tape or archive of your project, once you've transferred the video to your hard drive and put the DV tape in a safe place. Using a hard drive camcorder requires that you offload your shots onto your computer so that you can reuse the drive for more shooting. So, without going through the intentional process of backing up the footage you just offloaded to your computer, you don't have a backup copy.

This may be one of the reasons that MiniDV is still widely used and that hard drive systems haven't taken over. Beyond that, it is always a risky business to offer consumers a myriad of choices (Alvin Toffler coined the term "overchoice" for this phenomenon) and hope that the market will decide which format will win out. In any case, if you already have a digital camcorder in any of these mentioned formats, you should do fine (just remember to archive your footage if it's not a MiniDV format). If you haven't purchased a digital camcorder yet, make sure you think about the format you want before you get to the store.

Choosing High Definition or Standard Definition

Standard definition (SD) is the format we were all used to up to just a few years ago. When you look at a high definition (HD or HiDef) television (whether it be plasma, LCD, or any other type), you are looking at a screen aspect ratio of 16:9. It is more rectangular (widescreen) in appearance, as opposed to the square-looking standard definition aspect ratio of 4:3 (see Figure 5.2 for a comparison).

Figure 5.2

HD has not only higher resolution than SD, but also it has a widescreen (16:9) aspect ratio.

High definition also has a higher resolution—it looks crisp, clear, clean—with deeper, richer colors and more depth. This is terrific for viewing video on large screen television sets. But that is the crux of the following question: Where and how will your video be used? If it is ultimately going to be shown on a large screen, the HD could be the way to go. After all, most new cameras are HD, and the format is rapidly taking over in home television setups.

But if you are really targeting the Internet as your venue, HD might be overkill. The downside of HD is that its large file size requirements demand large storage devices, even with the compression that is necessary to further reduce the file size. Furthermore, even the standard definition digital files from your camcorder will have to be compressed in order to be small enough for Internet viewing.

All things considered, the SD format could be considered plenty enough resolution for web viewing. If you are planning other venues or showings on large screens, you might consider HD, which can serve that purpose as well as be compressed for use on the Internet.

Choosing the Right Camcorder Setup

Whatever format you choose, here are some other necessities for your digital camcorder. The inputs and outputs labeled A through E can be seen in Figure 5.3.

▷ A built-in microphone

▷ External microphone input (A)

▷ Audio inputs/outputs (line level) (B)

▷ FireWire port (C)

▷ USB port (D)

▷ An earphone jack (E)

▷ Auto-focus that can be manually overridden

▷ A zoom lens and, if possible, the ability to switch lenses

Figure 5.3
Typical camcorder connections should include audio I/O, FireWire, USB, mic jack, and earphone jack.

Choosing the Best Computer Setup

Digital audio, digital video, and the Internet—all are centered on the computer. Without that particular part of the equation, there is no discussion about making music videos and posting them on the Internet—not in terms of present-day production processes, that is. So, the computer is not only necessary, it is really the "brains" of the production (besides your own brain, that is).

Mac or PC?

There is not enough room here to discuss the ongoing controversy of Macs versus PCs as to which computer platform is better. Even if there were room, the debate would never be conclusive. Both platforms have powerful processors and both have software available for music and video production, not to mention film and video production.

In the creative community, there does seem to be a propensity for the Mac platform, and if you are in the market for a computer, it deserves careful consideration. If, on the other hand, you already have a PC, there is no reason it can't be the center of your production studio. The whole controversy is "solved" in Figure 5.4.

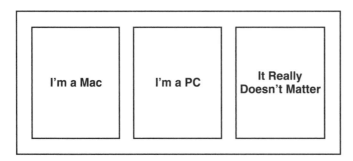

Figure 5.4
When it comes to creating music videos, the whole Mac versus PC controversy is finally over. You can choose the one that best fits your particular needs.

Horse…er…Computing Power

The basic rule is this: The more computing power you can get for your audio and video projects, the better. Developments in this area are taking place so fast that it's hard to say what the "latest, greatest" hardware might be by the time you read this. At the time of this writing, however, most audio and video professionals and semi-professionals are using PCs with clock speeds in the 2.8 to 3.0 GHz range. This is also the day of the multi-core processor, with four or eight cores being commonplace in editing suites. Your project can be completed on a computer with less horsepower, but more powerful machines will contribute to overall productivity—the time it takes to process things, as well as the overall stability of your software. Get the best that you can afford and remember—something more powerful is always around the corner anyway, so there's no need to wait.

Big Hunks of Data for RAM and Storage

Digital media, both audio and video, require a large amount of storage space. If you're creating a new song for your project, you'll need a lot of space for your audio files. You will be needing storage for your master video files. But that's just the beginning. Each of these types of files will require multiple revisions, edits, versions, and so on. In addition, you will need compressed versions of these versions, and at that, you'll likely be experimenting with different compression methods to get the best results possible.

These things used to be measured in terms of megabytes, but with the heavy requirements of audio and video, you need to think in terms of gigabytes. The computers themselves have speed measurements in gigahertz and require RAM in terms of gigabytes. So you need to make sure you have the horsepower and storage necessary to create and manage multi-media files.

Without compression, an hour of raw, uncompressed video may consume as much as 100GB of disk space. Just one hour of MiniDV footage will occupy about 13GB of hard disk space. Using compression will certainly require less, but remember that you need to have storage accommodations for all of the iterations previously mentioned.

Once you finish your production, much of it can be archived onto DVD, which can hold about 4.7GB of disc space. However, do not attempt to use DVD in place of a hard drive during the production process. The speed and access times of hard drives are necessary for full motion playback of video files.

Monitors, Interfaces, Cables, and More

Each computer environment is unique. Some things will differ depending on the location of the workstation. If you are set up in a commercial building or office, you may have more flexibility because of additional space. But even in a home studio environment, there are specific elements that are necessities and others that border on luxuries.

A dual-monitor system used to be a luxury, but today it is more commonplace because the prices for LCD monitors have come way down. Other necessities, such as a FireWire interface, will vary according to price yet they perform the same essential function. And cables, no matter how small your workstation is, are never too plentiful.

Monitors

Dual-monitor systems are fast becoming the norm, not only in video production suites, but also in audio production setups. With the vast array of tools and process-specific screens involved in production, two monitors are almost a necessity. The word *almost* is key here, because although it would be ideal to have two monitors at your disposal, it's very possible to create incredible work using only one monitor. As with other tools, budget will often dictate what you will have in your arsenal.

If you have a two-monitor setup, you may opt to have your main working environment on one monitor and other supporting windows on the other. Or you may choose to have all of your software windows on one and all of your files on the other. The flexibility of having two monitors creates a variety of possibilities that are up to your particular preference.

In audio and video production suites, you will rarely find monitors less than 20 inches in size. So if you're going to get a monitor (or monitors) for the first time, opt for larger screens if your budget allows for it. You will never regret that choice. Figure 5.5 shows an Apple Cinema Display that measures 23 inches diagonally.

Figure 5.5
If you can't afford a two-monitor system, try to get a large monitor such as this Apple 23-inch Cinema Display.

Interfaces

Aside from the standard requirements for cables that interconnect computers with keyboards, mice, monitors, printers, and speakers, there is the matter of the connections between your computer and audio peripherals, as well as the connections between your computer and video peripherals.

The most common type of connection for this purpose is known as FireWire. (FireWire is also known by another name, 1394.) A FireWire connection can be made directly between your computer and a digital video camera, assuming that both devices have a FireWire port (most of them do). A FireWire port can be added to your computer if it doesn't already have one. The connection between your computer and audio devices is a bit more complex and requires a FireWire *interface*, not simply a cable. Figure 5.6 shows a PreSonus FireWire interface that can accommodate both audio and video connections.

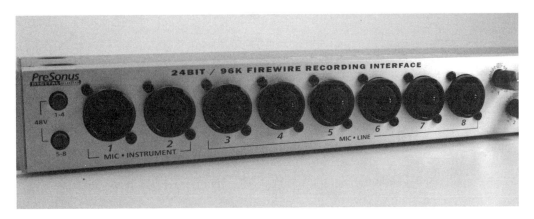

Figure 5.6
A FireWire interface can handle your studio's audio and video connections.

FireWire is the most common means of transferring data from your camera to the computer. FireWire interfaces usually have more than one port, so there should be no problem setting up your interface to handle all the tasks you need.

Cables

There's an old saying: "You can never have enough _____." You can fill in just about any word in the blank space, but in this case, you will fill in the blank with the word "cables." No matter how many cables you have, you're just one short of the exact cable you need. This is where redundancy—having duplicate cables—as well as excess—having more cables than you think you'll need—come into play.

The following list includes some cables you'll want to have around:

▷ FireWire

▷ USB

▷ Audio I/O

This is just the tip of the iceberg. When you're out on a shoot, make sure you have a collection of cables (possibly in a dedicated camera bag) that includes the following additions to the ones in the preceding list:

▷ AC power cables and extension cords

▷ Headphone extension cables

▷ RCA cables (long ones, 12 feet or more)

▷ Microphone cables including XLR, 14 inch, and mini-plug (⅛ inch)

▷ USB extension cables

▷ FireWire extension cables

If you are planning to have a computer on location, make a list of all the computer cables you'll need and, if possible, buy duplicates of each one.

Finally, you'll need adapters in addition to the cables mentioned previously, such as:

▷ XLR to ¼ inch (female to male, male to female)

▷ RCA to ¼ inch (female to male, male to female)

▷ Mini-plug to ¼ inch (female to male, male to female)

The list goes on, but you get the idea. Your guideline for this process is another old saying: "Hope for the best, but prepare for the worst." You don't want a little cable or adaptor to hold up your production, especially when other people are on the set, waiting for you.

Choosing the Best Software

In the olden days—which I calculate as eight or nine years ago—the tools available for audio and video production were primarily in the form of hardware. Recording studios, whether on a commercial street or in an empty bedroom—housed wall-to-wall black boxes of audio, MIDI, and outboard effects gear. Consoles were as big as refrigerators, although they were incapable of keeping one's beer cold. Computers may or may not have been present, but they certainly weren't used the way they are today.

Audio Software

Just as the Mac and PC present two points of view on what hardware to use, many competing companies present the same battle when it comes to which software to use. The software can mean your main sequencer (for your DAW), or it can mean samples—your sound libraries. The bottom line is that there are tons of great software packages to choose from.

Sequencers or Digital Audio Workstation Software

On the Mac side, the two main contenders are Apple's Logic Pro 9 and MOTU's Digital Performer 7. I say "main contenders" because they are the most widely used, but are by no means the *only* choices you have for Mac DAW software. The cool thing about both of these packages is that they interface very easily with Apple's Final Cut software.

The line-up of DAW software is extensive and is presented in the following table in no particular order (so that I can't be accused of having favorites—even though I do).

DAW Software

Software Title	Manufacturer	Platform
Logic Pro/Logic Studio	Apple	Mac
Digital Performer	MOTU (Mark of the Unicorn)	Mac
Sonar 8	Cakewalk	Windows
Cubase 4	Steinberg	Mac/Windows
Live 7	Ableton	Mac/Windows
Acid Pro 7	Sony	Windows
Producer 8	FL Studio	Windows
Tracktion 3	Mackie	Windows
Nuendo	Steinberg	Mac/Windows

Plug-Ins

There are two main categories of plug-ins: software or virtual instruments, and audio processing plug-ins. The list of these plug-ins is so huge that they can fill up an entire catalog (and, it so happens, they do fill up entire catalogs). If you've ever seen the catalog from Sweetwater Sound, you know what I mean.

When you evaluate plug-ins, you have to consider platform compatibility (does it work with your computer *and* its CPU chip?) and software compatibility (does it work with your host sequencer or DAW?). The list of software instruments includes everything from orchestral instruments to hip-hop loops to ethnic vocals. Audio processing can include limiters, compressors, reverbs, and mastering and noise-reducing software.

Your task is to figure out which ones you need and to make sure they work with your particular system. Because of the tremendous amount, diversity, and technical issues associated with plug-ins, I will not go into any more detail here. Utilize the web and your network of musician friends to determine the must-haves if you don't already have the already-haves in your arsenal. And of course, you can always use Google to search for the types of plug-ins you want and narrow the search to your particular platform (computer).

Video Software

There are many software packages for video production and editing, but as in the rest of this book, I'm focusing on what might be more suitable for a typical music video production.

The main packages in use today are Final Cut (Pro and Express versions), Adobe Premiere, and Avid Express. Avid has an extensive product line-up, and most of it is likely too expensive for what you're trying to achieve. Adobe Premiere has been around for a long time but is not as widely used as both versions of Apple's Final Cut software. Apple also makes iMovie, but it is likely not a good choice for your purposes. Many recent "improvements" in iMovie have also eliminated certain necessities. For example, in the most recent (as of this writing) version, 8.0, the capability of manually adjusting audio levels is not there. I can't understand the reasoning behind this, but having this capability is an absolute necessity when you are balancing music, voice, and effects tracks. iMovie is more powerful than one might imagine, and I'm sure somebody, somewhere, has created a decent music video using it. But I would recommend nothing less than Final Cut Express (shown in Figure 5.7) for any serious video work—and if you can afford it, Final Cut Pro.

For a comprehensive look at the latest video software, you might try Googling "video editing software." You will not only get links to specific software solutions, but also reviews and comparisons of multiple video-editing products as well.

Video editing is known as a nonlinear process, because with random access disk drives, you can locate and edit at any point in the program and not disturb the rest of the sequence. In the "old days," before nonlinear software, tape machines (linear) were used along with a variety of devices—switchers, TBCs (time-based correctors), mixers, and others—in order to achieve what you can do today with a laptop computer.

Most video-editing software programs have a basic architecture that includes a preview window, a program window, a bin for audio and video files, and a timeline. The timeline is where you place—or sequence—your clips in the order that you want. You can usually trim or fine-edit these clips right on the timeline. You may also be able to add effects, such as transitions, fades, or wipes—from one scene to another.

Figure 5.7
A screenshot of Apple's Final Cut software.

The timeline provides at least one stereo audio track, but usually you'll have the capability to accommodate several tracks of audio and even multiple tracks of video. Additional video tracks are used for video effects such as superimposing titles, video overlays, and so on. Multiple audio tracks will accommodate your stereo music track along with any other sound effects you may want to lay in.

You get into the nitty-gritty details of using audio and video software as it relates to making music videos in Chapter 9, "Post-Production".

Choosing a
Video Style

MUSIC VIDEOS ARE LIKE SNOWFLAKES—no two are alike. Okay, maybe a lot of them are alike in certain ways, but everyone strives to make theirs different. Just like clothing, videos have a certain style. Although all of them are videos that consist of music and visuals, they are conceived, created, and expressed in a certain mood or feeling, simply by the way they are put together.

A video style will generally correspond to a music genre. It would be odd to see a country music video portrayed by musicians who had all the visual characteristics and attitudes of a hip hop group. It might be odd, indeed, but not impossible. That's the tricky part about finding your style—you want to identify with your genre and fit into the expectations of your audience, yet you want to add a touch of originality so that you are more than a copy cat act. It's easier said than done, and if there were a formula for doing it, you'd end up being "formula"—something you should avoid.

The Medium Is the Message

Marshall McLuhan is an author whose works are often a main part of college classes in communication theory. He is well known for coining phrases such as "the medium is the message," meaning that the form of a medium embeds itself in the message, creating a symbiotic relationship by which the medium influences how the message is perceived. He also coined the phrase "global village," a term describing the way that electronic communication has "shrunken" the size of the entire world into village proportions because information is transmitted and consumed instantly. Remarkably, these observations came well before the Internet and World Wide Web.

The "medium is the message" is something to consider as you determine your visual identity and video style, for the medium itself has just as much importance (if not more) than the content it carries. In your case, the medium is video, and more specifically, it is a music video.

It is not difficult to ponder how much this idea applies to a music video. If it weren't for the nature of the ubiquitous video format, music videos would not even exist. Video brought culture and counterculture into everyone's living rooms. It is front-and-center in the media-consuming lives of most people on the planet. It made its entrance during the lifetimes of the Baby Boomers, and more recently, to the X, Y, and you-name-it generations, making the consumption of video as common and natural as driving a car or reading a newspaper.

Now, with the video medium in the hands of the prosumer, it is even more of a symbiotic relationship. For a long time, anyone could watch a music video. Now, anyone can produce, direct, and star in one. It has empowered artists and musicians as much as it previously empowered businesses and corporations.

Finding Your Style in a World of Overchoice

Although I refer to him in a few other places, this book is not about Alvin Toffler, yet another great concept of his (that is very relevant) is that of "overchoice." He noted a long time ago that the expanding universe of goods and services was creating a phenomenon in which there are almost too many choices in our present-day world. Think of the boxes of cereal lined up on your supermarket shelf. It's overchoice—maybe even overchoice gone mad.

A Brief History of Music Videos

Music videos came of age in the 1980s. The first major channel for broadcasting this art form was a cable channel, namely MTV, followed later by VH1. As music videos developed, more emphasis was placed on storyline and visual effects, essential ingredients that are discussed several times in this book.

Perhaps no one had more influence on music videos than Michael Jackson. His 1983 music video of "Thriller" was 14 minutes long. Although many point out the price tag of the extensive production, somewhere in the neighborhood of a half a million dollars, the true historic value is that the video created a new standard for all that followed. It's true that music video production values and price tags increased, but so did the emphasis on story, plot, acting, and overall professionalism.

In 1985, MTV spun off VH1, essentially another music video channel meant to appeal to a slightly older demographic with a somewhat "softer" music line up. Today, music videos have another distribution method with the Internet. This began with many videos showing up on YouTube (and subsequently removed, to some extent, due to the objections of copyright owners) and continues with web versions of MTV, VH1, and other music video websites.

The concept of overchoice can be applied to the numerous styles of music as well. The pile of CDs in Figure 6.1 would represent a tiny fraction of the amount of music styles available today. In the "old days," you could select from a handful of genres in music—pop, jazz, classical, country, and so on. Today, the list of genres has expanded to encompass styles within styles, and genres within genres.

Figure 6.1
These CDs represent a small fraction of all the music styles to choose from.

Here is just one example of what a list of music genres might look like today:

Adult Alternative	Latin
Adult Contemporary	New Age
Blues	Christian
Rock—Alternative	Country
Rock—Classic	Country Rock
Rock—Hard	Country Crossover
Rock—Indie	R&B
Rock—Contemporary	Reggae
Heavy Metal	World
Folk	Ambient
Electronic/Dance	Acid Jazz
Hip Hop/Rap	Classical
House	Disco
Industrial	Trance
Pop	

Did I leave anyone out? I probably did. This is only an example list. There are other genres and other genres within these genres. For example, Heavy Metal can really be broken into further sub-genres, such as Death Metal, Thrash Metal, Black Metal, Power Metal, Progressive Metal, Gothic Metal, Doom Metal, Alternative Metal, Glam Metal, Industrial Metal, Sludge, Stoner, and Speed Metal—not to mention (hold onto your seats, ladies and gentlemen), Christian Metal. So, even with the preceding extensive list, there are many more sub-genres, each with their own particular style, within the main genre.

The question is: Where do you fit in within all of this? What is *your* genre? What is *your* style of music?

Perhaps you're thinking that you don't fit in with any of these categories. You don't like to be put in a little box with a little label. Your music is completely original, right? Wrong.

All music is derivative. I know, you probably resent that statement because your music is *totally* original. It's so original, in fact, that it defies categorization. You can't even put a label on it. And while you might think this is a good thing, wait until the marketing department tries to promote your music. They're going to want to put *some* sort of label on it, or else they can't communicate to the world what you are all about (see Figure 6.2).

Figure 6.2
Where does your style fit in? Are you aware of the other styles on the market?

It's not a bad thing to admit that your music is "sort of like (fill in the blank), with a slight touch of (fill in the blank)," and so on. As a matter of fact, it's a *good* thing to be able to position yourself in the marketplace. And when you can do that, you can also get a clearer picture of what it is you want to communicate—not only with your music, but also with your music video.

You will want your music video to express your particular *style* of music. This is not to say that you cannot push the envelope and break new ground in a particular genre, using a new spin or sporting a new style. Hopefully, you can. However, try to be realistic about it and realize that you are not reinventing the wheel.

Just as it is said by some of the judges on American Idol, you can take a song "and make it your own." You can do that with your music—and you can do that with your music video.

Matching Aesthetics of Music and Visuals

How do you go about creating, conveying, and projecting your particular style?

You steal it from others.

Okay, okay—please don't send cards and letters complaining about the suggestion of stealing from others. Let me put it another way. For you to have a *starting point* for understanding a particular style, you need to know what everyone else has done before you. You wouldn't, for example, create a Country music video with your group wearing all black clothing, chains, and sporting piercings and tattoos all over their bodies. Nor would you have a Heavy Metal band wearing cowboy gear. Not that there's any law against it. I just want you to be successful, that's all.

How do you know what everyone else has done up until now? As stated in a previous chapter, you do your homework—you watch and study tons of music videos, keeping aware of your state of mind. Sometimes you will get caught up in the music video itself, enjoying what you're watching. That's fine, but you also must keep an analytical frame of mind so that you are actually doing your homework. Take notes. Discuss what you see with others in your band or on your team.

Then you might consider having a brainstorming session to discuss what you might do to make the *style* your own. Decide if it might make sense to wear:

▷ Leg warmers with your outfit

▷ Your shorts *over* your pants

▷ A bustiere and spike heels

▷ Your hat backwards

Can you see where I'm going with this? These are all things that others have done that were previously unheard of. The queen of this in the musical arena is Madonna, who has not only done these types of things once, but many, many times.

However, for the most part, what she and others have done stylistically was not necessarily done randomly or unplanned. There are exceptions, of course, such as a time in the recent past in which someone put on a pair of Hush Puppies and before long, it became a trend. (Read Malcolm Gladwell's book, *The Tipping Point,* which examines the social epidemics around us, for more on this phenomenon.) In the case of the viral spread and rising popularity of Hush Puppies, there wasn't any prior planning involved. Nevertheless, you can influence culture intentionally or unintentionally by creating an epidemic (stylistically) of your own—and doing it through the medium of music videos is a great way to do it.

Exactly *how* you do it is up to you.

Shooting

Options

THERE'S MORE THAN ONE WAY to pet a cat—and there's more than one way to shoot a music video. In addition to the different methods of shooting the video, there are combinations of those methods. I would say that the number of ways to shoot the video are limited only by your imagination, but that would sound like a cliché. So I won't say that.

The options you have for shooting your music video come under two main headings. One deals with the technical aspects, including the number of cameras you're using and the different ways in which you can record the audio. The other over-arching category has to do with style of video you want to create. Will it be a live video of a live performance? Will it be a dramatic story, intercutting between lip-synced performances and cut-away or B-roll footage? Chapter 6, "Choosing a Video Style," goes into detail about choosing a video style in terms of genre and the look, feel, and identity you want to portray. This chapter discusses style as it relates to the options you might choose for shooting the video and recording the audio, depending on the type of video you are creating.

Performing Live

Probably the easiest way to shoot a music video is to literally shoot a video of your band—or of your act—performing live and then call it a day. One camera. One band. One song, beginning to end. As you can see, there is one potential drawback, and that is boredom.

Now, if the band is the Rolling Stones or an artist of that caliber and fame, then maybe this idea will fly. But for us up-and-comers, the song (and performance) would not only have to be extremely good, it would also need some buzz around it. You see, before the Rolling Stones were the Rolling Stones, most people didn't give them a second glance. The "here's my band performing at the Long Beach Battle of the Bands last year" type of video is more like a home movie than a music video, and you know how those home movies can be.

Now, before you send in those cards and letters telling me how crazy I am and how much nerve I have saying something like this, please stop. First of all, I'm talking in general terms about most cases. And second of all, I am one never to say "never." You'll see that thread of belief tied together throughout this book. If your music video is simply one live take of your act performing a song from beginning to end, and people love it, more power to you. Still, there are some things to keep in mind even when creating this kind of music video, especially if it is recorded at a concert or other type of live event. (I introduce the topic of recording live events here, and then go into more detail in Chapter 8, "The Video Process: Pre-Production and the Shoot," where I discuss the live multi-camera shoot and recording live audio.)

One important point to keep in mind is that you need to feed your camcorder a direct recording of the audio, usually from the output of the house mixer, and *not* from the microphone. Using the camcorder's built-in microphone is not a good idea, that is, unless you want poor quality audio. Record the audio separately the best way you can and, if necessary, sync it up later. And when I say not to use the microphone input of the camcorder, I'm saying avoid using that audio for your *final* audio. You *do*, however, want to record the audio through the audio inputs of the camcorder so that, at the very least, you have a reference point for synchronizing everything later, especially if you plan to sync up with a separate recording of the event.

You can improve a live video by at least a notch by shooting with additional cameras and by using more than one angle. You can also add cameras beyond those two, if you want, and include wide shots, close-ups, and audience-reaction shots to create alternative clips that correspond to the same point of time within the song.

Again, you can record the main audio directly into the camcorder inputs, and sync up the clips later at your heart's content. You can have the second and/or third cameras record "wild"—meaning that you could use their microphone inputs (or better yet, a higher-quality external microphone) to capture applause and other miscellaneous sounds. This type of shoot yields a professional look. In Figure 7.1, you can see how a feed from the house mixer to the audio inputs of the camcorder, along with second and third cameras recording wild audio, can be set up.

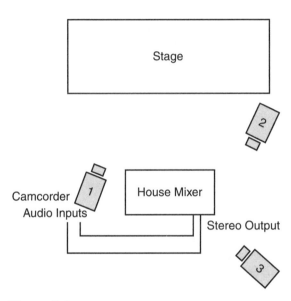

Figure 7.1
This diagram shows one possible setup for using three cameras to shoot a live concert for a music video.

Shooting a live performance is akin to shooting a documentary. You are, in essence, documenting the time and place of an event, and not a whole bunch more. As you will see in the discussion of other types of videos (story-driven videos and effect-laden videos), shooting a live performance will take you only so far. More often than not, you will want to add some dressing or frosting to your presentation.

Shooting a "Mini-Movie"—
The Story-Driven Music Video

A long, long time ago—in a network television station not so far away (not from *my* house, anyway)—a young man had an idea for making music more interesting. It was long ago, for it was the 1970s, and the young man was me. I was a big fan of many of the great artists of that era, including Simon and Garfunkel. Every time I heard one of their songs, I could see moving pictures in my mind's eye. It isn't difficult to do this with their music, because their music is very "visual." It lends itself, easily, to a visual presentation.

I was working in the newsroom of CBS Television in Los Angeles. No, I wasn't a big shot or anything—quite the contrary. It was one of the very first jobs I ever had—I was a "runner" (also known as a "gopher"—go for this, go for that), and yet the job was very exciting for me at the beginning of my working years. I got that job because I knew Joe Landis, a producer at CBS. He got me in the door and proved to me early on that it *is* a matter of whom you know.

Many of the songs by Simon and Garfunkel could have made great music videos. But for some reason, I was hung up on a song of theirs called "Old Friends" from the album, *Bookends* (You can still order this great Simon and Garfunkel on Amazon.com, as shown in Figure 7.2). Here are the lyrics of the first verse:

> Old friends,
> Old friends
> Sat on their park bench
> Like bookends.
> A newspaper blown though the grass
> Falls on the round toes
> Of the high shoes
> Of the old friends.

You could be the worst video director on Planet Earth and still do a good job with those lyrics. It is truly a no-brainer. So, with this song in my head, I created a little presentation of how this could be made into a visual piece. Now, keep in mind there was no MTV at that time. Heck, there weren't even any videos at that time, except for the videos used in network broadcasting. There were no home videos or video rentals or cable television. (I told you it was a long, long time ago.)

Figure 7.2
The *Bookends* album by Simon & Garfunkel, circa 1968, is available today on Amazon.com.

So I made a storyboard type of presentation of "Old Friends," even though I didn't know how it might be used—in other words, what the delivery medium would eventually be. Back then I could visualize a regular weekly show, perhaps, with a group of songs presented in this visual style. Yes, I know, we have these now, and they're called music videos, and they run 'em around the clock. I could picture it back then.

But my friend, Joe, at CBS couldn't picture it. He gave me a nice pat on the back and sent me on my way. So, I thought to myself, "How silly…who would want to see songs made into visual stories anyway?" And there you have it, ladies and gentlemen. No, I'm not saying that I was the inventor of the music video before there were music videos. After all, I didn't do anything about "Old Friends" or anything else for that matter after Joe had passed on it. I *could* have been an inventor of the music video, but I didn't pursue the idea. And if you don't know it by now, perseverance is a requirement in the entertainment business.

Can you imagine us
Years from today,
Sharing a park bench quietly?
How terribly strange
To be seventy.
Old friends,
Memory brushes the same years
Silently sharing the same fears.

Ah, so sweet. So visual. Such story-driven music.

Whether the music comes first or whether an idea that spawns the music and the visuals to go with it comes first, the result is the same: story-driven music. A story-driven music video is a mini-movie of sorts. You can write a song; then later you can write a script and hire the actors, the director, and the production crew to produce a mini-movie that we now call a music video. Or you might conceive the whole package right from the start and create it that way. Regardless, you end up with a three- or four-minute music video.

Combining Live Performance with Story-Driven Videos

This section's title describes the majority of all music videos—a combination of a live studio performance with a scripted, story-driven production. In the majority of videos, you'll see three or four seconds of a band performing and then see a cut to the band members (or actors) acting out the part that the lyrics are describing. Then you will likely see a cut back to the band performing. The video may stay on these shots for even shorter amounts of time than three or four seconds. It is not uncommon today to see clips that are one second or less, whether they are live performance shots or scripted segments. Actually, many have described the "MTV Generation" as baby boomers who grew up on the quick cuts and rock n' roll of the seventies and eighties. In a land long ago and far away (say, before 1965), the pace of visuals in a movie or television production was much, much slower—so much so, that many in today's generation might fall asleep from boredom if subjected to such a show.

Where to Begin

If you did your earlier homework assignment (in the sidebar of Chapter 3, "Music Video Cookbook: The Ingredients") of watching hours of music videos, you may have noticed a variation of the live/scripted video formats. But before you take out your camcorder—even before you start writing your script—keep in mind the variety of live/story-driven videos you can create:

▷ **The standard:** Videos of this kind begin with the band (or artist), cut to a scripted segment and back to the band, and so on, alternating throughout, as described in the preceding section. Often the intro to the song will be scripted and then cut to the act at the beginning of the vocal.

▷ **The standard plus:** This type of video is like the preceding one, but with a dozen or so costume changes within the context of the same song. Sometimes the artist will be lip syncing, sometimes not.

▷ **The setup:** This type of video begins with a story segment as a setup, perhaps 30 seconds to a minute long; then it cuts to the band, and back again.

▷ **Animation:** Here there are no real video images of the artist, only computer animation or hand-drawn images.

▷ **Stop motion:** These videos have a variety of sub-flavors—combined with performance, not combined with performance, or blended with several types of formats.

▷ **Green screen:** These videos have a completely fabricated "set" created by computer animation combined with the act's video footage.

▷ **Motion picture soundtrack:** If you're lucky enough to have a song placed in a movie, you might also be lucky enough to make a music video that intercuts between your song and clips from the film. These soundtracks are usually reserved for major acts, but they aren't out of the realm of possibility.

▷ **The combo:** Any combination of the previously mentioned.

Understanding the Difference
Between Film Scores and Music Videos

This might be a good time to take a look at the difference between a film score and a music video. It is interesting to note that these two disciplines come from opposite ends of the spectrum. As I've been discussing, a live performance and a story-driven music video are based upon one major element—the music. Although I've mentioned a few different types of productions, one thing remains the same. The music is the real "driver" of the music video. That's where it all starts, and that's where it all ends.

When a composer is scoring a film, the opposite is true. The visual—the story—drives the music. The task here is to make the music fit the visual. The music takes on two primary roles:

▷ To enhance the emotional context of the scene

▷ To help move the story along

In a music video, the emotional context is already there in the form of the music and the lyrics. In a film, there may, in fact, be a story with some emotional context, but when scored effectively, the music really brings the emotional context to new highs (or lows, depending on the scene). Take out the music and two things are likely to happen: You will not have as much depth of emotion in the film, and the movie will plug slowly along, seemingly taking forever to reach the end. The musical score addresses both of these issues very well.

Again, before you send in those cards and letters saying that I've lost my mind—yes, there *are* exceptions. One example can be found in nature-based videos that are typically accompanied by new age or ambient music. In this case, the visuals and music are of equal "weight," and it would be difficult to call a clear "winner" in terms of who's driving what (see Figure 7.3 for "driving" directions). These are relaxing, healing videos that are essentially *scored*—the visuals come first, and the composer sets it all to music. So although there are exceptions, there are generally rules, and sometimes those rules are broken.

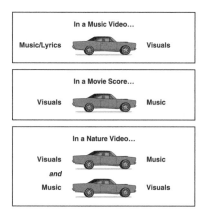

Figure 7.3
Who's Driving What?

What is interesting about the overall comparison is that the audio tool chests of a songwriter (doing a music video) and a composer (creating a film score) are the same. The DAW, the sequencing software; the virtual instruments; and the outboard gear can all be found in either studio. (Recall that DAW stands for Digital Audio Workstation software, as explained in Chapters 1, "The Process," and 5, "Tools for Do-It-Yourselfers".) If you fall under the DIY (Do-It-Yourself) classification for the video aspect of the production, the only additions might be the camcorder, the editing software, and other items directly related to video production.

The Video Process:

Pre-Production and the Shoot

I F, BY NOW, YOU HAVE SELECTED the song you are going to use for your music video and you have it "in the can" (that's Hollywood talk for "it is complete and ready to go"), then the next thing you're going to be tempted to do is start shooting. Don't do that—not yet, anyway.

As I mention in Chapter 7, "Shooting Options," a major consideration before you do anything is determining what type of music video you're going to produce. It may be a recording of the song during a live concert or performance. It may be a story-driven song that is expressed with lots of visuals, real or abstract. Your choice will affect what type of preparation is needed. A live recording may require less formal preparation (although it still requires some planning and preparation nonetheless). I encourage you to read the following sections on preparation regardless of the type of video you are planning to create. A lot of this information is applicable to music videos that are primarily a live shoot of a performance or event.

Preparing for the Shoot

There is a natural excitement inherent in the desire to shoot a music video. Ideas are spinning in your head. You can visualize some of the scenes so vividly that it almost feels like they've been shot already. You can even imagine sitting down with a group of friends and showing it to them after it's been posted on the web. How far away can stardom be, at this point of the game?

Well, stardom could be extremely far away if you don't take advantage of Step 1—Preparation.

1. Preparation

Here's a homework assignment. Go rent or buy *Close Encounters of the Third Kind* by director Steven Spielberg. Do this whether or not you've already seen the film. Watch it from beginning to end and ask yourself these questions:

 ▷ Is every shot precisely framed as if it were a composition of a professional photograph or painting?

 ▷ How did Spielberg orchestrate those incredible camera moves? How can a camera even move that way?

 ▷ Are the lead characters, from the suburban couple to the little boy who gets abducted to the Neary children, expertly cast? Are they totally, inescapably perfectly cast?

 ▷ Is the music scored well throughout? Is it just a coincidence that the music, which is key to communicating with the aliens, is woven throughout the score in a variety of interesting variations—some subtle and some pronounced?

If you are getting the drift here, then you know that none of this could have happened without extensive preparation and pre-planning. These elements do not happen by accident. This is not to say that you won't sometimes end up with footage that was not planned but is nevertheless excellent. Those types of accidents do happen.

Although you are not making a full-length motion picture, many of the principles are the same. That's why, in addition to watching lots of music videos, you can get a very good education by watching films and reading books and magazines on filmmaking. However, when you watch movies for your own educational purposes, the trick is to not get hooked into the story (that is, movie) thereby losing track of your analytical thinking process.

Creating the Script

One difference between a full-length motion picture and a music video has to do with the script. The lyrics of the song already provide a great deal of the script. Lyrics are a basic roadmap for what scenes will be acted out in the video, at least from a conceptual standpoint. Lyrics are, however, not the whole enchilada. You may know conceptually what you want to show, but that doesn't provide you with any of the detail—hence, the need for scripts, storyboards, director's notes, and so on.

Types of Scripts

A variety of software programs are on the market that help you lay out a script. Some of them are overkill for the purpose of a music video, and some may prove useful. Some examples of screenwriting software include Final Draft, Movie Magic, Five Sprockets, Hollywood Screenwriter, and more. A simpler version of screenwriting software can be found in Movie Outline 3, but even at that, this program probably has a ton of features that you would never use in a music video script.

At the very least, you can create a simple script based on the old style audio/visual or slideshow presentations, which might look something like Figure 8.1.

Visual

Close-Up of Danny Dismal

Cut to Rhythm Guitarist

Audio

From song lyrics

Second verse:

"I told you I loved you but I couldn't come over

I'm in a new band though we only do covers"

Instumental only

Sound of rhythm guitar:

Bring up volume of rhythm guitar as camera slowly zooms in

Hold until Danny starts singing again

Figure 8.1
Even an old style slideshow script can be repurposed for a music video script.

In the case of a music video, the narration is replaced by the song's lyrics. If four lines of the lyrics were to be conveyed by one distinct scene and the next few lyrics were conveyed by another scene, each would get its own "box" and accompanying description. It's sort of a very simplified combination of script and storyboard.

This covers the basics, but more is needed to describe scenes that are not inherent in the lyrics. For example, if the written lyric were "Our love is strong, it survives the storms," the visual might be the vocalist singing that line in a live or taped performance. Or it might be a completely different visual of the singer holding on for dear life to the sail of a boat in the midst of a strong storm (that is, if budget allowed). The visual might be represented in a number of different ways—and it is the function of the script to say (as precisely as possible) how the visual is to be executed in the final video.

In a typical movie script, one page might be the equivalent of one minute of actual motion picture time. This varies widely and is only a general average. But a typical movie script has a completely different format consisting of the scene description, the character(s), the dialogue, the action taking place, and so on. Here is a typical format for a movie script.

FADE IN:
THE SIXTH STRING OF AN ELECTRIC GUITAR
is plucked with force. It is apparently out of tune. Fingers twist the tuning peg.
The string is plucked again, twice.

DANNY (O.S.)
How does that sound to you?

RANDY (O.S.)
Are you nuts? Can't you hear how out-of-tune that is?

TWO MEN
sit on a low wall outside a Hollywood club, bundled in sweaters against a cool L.A. wind, holding guitars, tuning up as best they can.

SUPERIMPOSE: APRIL, 2009.

RANDY BURROWS is the big one, an athlete in a previous life, a bit of a tire around the middle. DANNY SULLIVAN is slimmer, more sophisticated, and brighter.

> DANNY
>
> The reason it sounds out-of-tune, Randy, is because it *is*!

> RANDY
>
> Heck no. It is not. I've been playing a lot longer than you, pal!

Danny plays a lead guitar line. He's not bad. But Randy shakes his head.

> DANNY
>
> You must be deaf.

While Danny plays, Randy reaches over and gives Danny's tuning peg a twist to the right. The string breaks and Randy smiles.

> DANNY
>
> Oh no you didn't! You didn't just break my string!

> RANDY
>
> Danny, I'd be doing everyone a favor by breaking all of your strings!

> Randy starts twisting all the tuning pegs on Danny's guitar. They both start laughing.

As the sun sets over North Hollywood, California, a neon sign lights up behind Randy and Danny — "The Palomino Club"

HARD CUT TO:

TELEVISION SCREEN SHOWING A ROCK CONCERT

The footage is shaky, handheld shots in black and white, with lots of horizontal lines evident. A band's name is almost visible on the bass drum, but too blurry to read.

Script formats may be typical but they are not standardized—there will always be a few minor variations. Still, the main elements are as follows:

▷ Stage direction

▷ Character name

▷ Dialogue

▷ Parenthetical (direction to the actor just before dialogue)

▷ Action

▷ Other instructions, such as CUT TO, or STILL PHOTO, or BANG (sound effects)

It can be argued that a traditional move script format is overkill for a music video and that the simple slideshow format is better suited. That may be, but if you are writing for an opening segment or any other section that has a story-like feel to it, the typical film script format may be well suited to it.

If you use the traditional script format, the song lyrics can be substituted for the dialogue. If the clip you're showing at any given time is an existing shot of the act, you can simply indicate that, as shown in this example:

15 Band clip (sync)

This is an example where nothing specific about the shot is indicated, except that it should be in sync with whatever lyric is being sung at that particular point.

The next example shows how a script might read if you have a specific shot in mind or if you use an existing shot you've already identified.

16 EXT GIBSON AMPHITHEATER

Hear Today, Gone Tomorrow

Wide shot of the band, featuring lead singer

Sync

In this example, the script is showing Scene 16. It is a wide shot taken at the Universal Amphitheater of the band, Hear Today, Gone Tomorrow, featuring the lead singer.

Again, the lead singer is singing the lyric and the video clip is showing this in sync. Why must this be stated? The reason is simple. You could just as easily have a shot in which the camera pans up on the lead singer who is *not* singing at all. As you know from studying music videos, some clips—usually short clips—are inserted without the vocalist singing, until perhaps the following shot in which she is.

A script that describes video that hasn't been shot yet requires more detail. Here is one example of that scenario:

17 EXT GIBSON AMPHITHEATER

Hear Today, Gone Tomorrow

We see the band walking to the amphitheater, just before sunset

CAMERA: Pans left to right from band member 1 to lead singer, holds, and then finishes pan to band member 5

LYRICS:

I see the sun setting before my eyes

My tears are merging with the sky

This is just one example. Your script can always be customized to your needs as long as it is understandable to you later and to others on your team.

Beyond the Shoot

The script is your roadmap for your music video production. The song lyrics give you a big head start in knowing what you might do to create the video. But without preparation, from the simplest pondering of ideas to writing out detailed notes, a script cannot emerge.

The script will be with you from the time it is conceived and written to the final video master. It goes beyond the shoot and lasts into post-production. If you've ever seen a real script created for almost any purpose, I'm sure you've noticed many notes written in the margins as well as text crossed out and rewritten by hand, not to mention arrows, circles, and the occasional doodle.

The script also goes beyond your own needs and serves as a guideline for everyone else in the production—from the camera operator to the editor to the actors to the recording engineers (assuming that you're not doing *all* of these jobs yourself).

Creating a Storyboard

A storyboard is like a visual script. Many creative people are inclined to be more visual than others. Whether they are or not, the storyboard provides the crew with the type of instruction that words can only begin to tell. If the storyboard is a good one, there will be little difference in the way it originally looks and the way the final scenes look, especially in terms of framing and composition. Sometimes on the actual set, ideas emerge that vary from the storyboard, which is fine. But generally speaking, the storyboard can be a great asset for everyone on the team. Figure 8.2 shows an example of a storyboard.

Figure 8.2
A storyboard may contain only pictures,
or it may have descriptive text as well.

The storyboard is a natural evolution from the script. Among other things, a storyboard tells who or what is in the scene. It also indicates the camera moves and can indicate how to frame a particular scene.

Although it seems a natural fit that storyboards are used in an animation sequence, they are just as useful and necessary for live action. Storyboards can be very simple, such as stick figures, or very elaborate—sometimes looking like a finished comic book. It's wise to base your expectations for your storyboard on what you—or someone in your crew—are capable of producing.

Creating Animatics

Animatics are sort of like storyboards on steroids. Animatics are storyboards that have been put to animation. The animation is usually rudimentary. In its simplest form, it might consist of a series of hand-drawn visuals that are sequenced in order of each scene. Although the drawings might be very basic, they still represent the essential part of the scene, including the desired camera angle. This presentation can be authored in any number of applications, from a simple PowerPoint presentation to one constructed in Final Cut Pro. The final output is usually in the form of a QuickTime movie, which is playable on both the PC and Mac platforms.

In addition to providing a better sense of timing than would be possible on a storyboard, an animatic can provide another distinct advantage—an audio track. Animatics audio tracks can accommodate a music temp track, which could be helpful for someone scoring a film or commercial. In the case of your music video, it will likely be the song itself. In other types of productions, there is also the possibility of including a narration track, sound effects, and so on.

A more sophisticated animatic might provide actual frames from an animation, assuming the music video contained animated sequences. It might include still shots as opposed to hand drawings. The bottom line is that an animatic can provide more of a sense of the desired outcome of an audio/visual piece. This might not be necessary in the case of your music video, depending primarily on how much you need to communicate your vision to other cast or crew members. That's another decision to add to your seemingly endless list of decisions. Regardless, if you can use any (or all) of the tools that are available for story development, your final product may be that much better, not to mention that it could speed up your entire production process (see Figure 8.3).

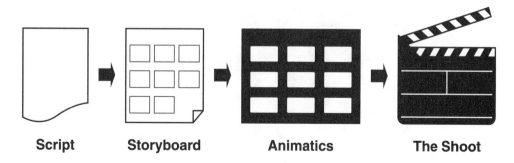

Script　　　**Storyboard**　　　**Animatics**　　　**The Shoot**

Figure 8.3
Using any or all of the available tools for story development can improve your production process.

Taking the Ad Hoc Approach

If you eliminate everything that's been discussed from the beginning of this chapter until now, you would essentially have an ad hoc approach to your production. That means no preparation, no script, and no storyboard.

You can probably guess what this author is thinking about this approach. (*Hint:* Not a good idea.) Even if you took the most basic of basic concepts for a music video—the live shoot— and decided not to add anything else to it, you would likely come up short in the editing room. Did you get a combination of long, medium, and close-up shots? Did you get additional footage to which you can cut away? What about the same scene from different angles? How about the sound—is it ready for high-quality playback?

As you may have already surmised, I'm one who understands rules can be broken. As such, maybe it is possible to create a music video this way and not have your audience fall asleep. After all, it is *possible.*

But what you may want to keep in mind is this: Today's music video audiences are fairly sophisticated. Remember, they were brought up during or after the MTV revolution. They all might qualify for ADD prescriptions. They've seen some very elaborate productions and special effects that are made with industrial light and some magic thrown in.

So, if you want to make a music video ad hoc style, go right ahead. But don't say I didn't warn you!

Shooting the Video

If you were to watch a professional camera crew at work, you might mistakenly come to the conclusion that shooting video is easy—that there's "nothing to it." This happens in other professions as well. When you watch gymnasts performing in a competition or dancers dancing in a show, the quality of their performances can easily create the illusion that there's nothing to it. That's largely because they are so talented. There may be years or even decades of experience behind what they're doing. As professionals approach mastery of their crafts, they appear to perform effortlessly.

The same can be said for shooting a music video. The process involves a lot more than "point-and-shoot." How far you want to take the craft and technicalities of video making or filmmaking is up to you (assuming that you are shooting the video yourself). In this chapter, I assume that you (or your videographer) have *some* experience with a camera. And, as in other chapters, I will keep the focus on shooting video as it relates to the making of a *music* video.

The Basics of Shooting Video

Providing an in-depth explanation of shooting quality videos is beyond the scope of this book. That said, there are hundreds of good books on the market that can help you with every aspect of video production. As a matter of fact, Course PTR has a selection of books that deals extensively with digital video and filmmaking (for more resources, see Appendix A). You can also find resources on the Internet—some of them free—that can help with some of the basics on video production.

The following sections focus on issues that will be of importance to you in making a music video. If you need help with camera techniques, lighting, and other core production issues, use whatever resources you can to get up to speed *before* you embark on producing your music video.

A Brief History of Syncing Audio and Picture

This history lesson will be briefer than you might expect. Rather than discuss all of the issues related to synchronization, I'm going to focus on how it relates to you, today, in the context of a music video.

In a galaxy a long, long time ago (although it was not far, far away), filmmakers needed to sync their audio to whatever sound was being recorded. In most productions, the film recorded the picture (only) while the audio was recorded separately, usually to a tape machine such as a Nagra recorder. To ensure that the scenes began exactly at the same moment, a clapper was filmed. You've likely seen this before, and you can see it now in Figure 8.4. The clapper is also known as a "clapper board" and sometimes is referred to as a "slate," which actually is the bottom part of the clapper that documents the scene, the date, the time, and so on.

Figure 8.4
This handy little device (a clapper) ensures that sound and picture begin exactly at the same time.

There is simplicity here that pays off in big rewards later. When editing the film, the exact moment that the arm of the clapper hits the body of the clapper (the slate), a sound (of a clap, oddly enough) is heard that later tells the editor how to line up the audio with the video. A bulky old machine, first invented in the 1920s, known as a Moviola, had a motor driving a reel with the film and another driving a mag strip with the audio. The clapper was an essential tool that made certain where the sync point was when lining up the film and the audio. Directors used the clapper as a reference point. Because the film and the audio could be adjusted separately, it was possible to move one (or both) reels around on their respective motors until all of it lined up—again, using the clapper or slate as the reference or sync point. Later, as technologies developed, the clapper was replaced by electronic signals, such as a light burst on the film coupled with a tone on the audio track. Same idea, just a bit more sophisticated.

Now, how does this relate to you in these modern, sophisticated times, when audio and video are recorded together? I'm glad you asked, because you're going to see how this "old" technology can benefit you today.

To Sync or Not to Sync

This question is posed on several different levels. Do you need to sync the video with the *recording of the song* when you shoot? Do you need to sync different camera footage of the same song with other footage of the song? Do you need to sync lips, musicians playing instruments, and even "wild" footage with the audio track?

The answer is *all of the above*. When you shoot your video, you need to have a master recording of the song on hand. When you shoot, play back the track and have the artist lip sync and, likewise, have the musicians copy all of their own moves. You would be wise to shoot one continuous take of the song from beginning to end for a *reference* track. That way, you'll always know who's doing what at any particular point in the song. It will also serve as "back-up" footage in the event that a particular part of the song that is shot doesn't work out later. If you're doing a multi-camera shoot, that's even better—but still shoot a take from beginning to end to use as a reference track.

The idea of using a syncing device, such as a clapper, is simply good practice. When you are in post-production and are using lots of different pieces of video, it makes sense to know exactly where they sync up to the audio track—an audio track that is different than the audio track you recorded during the shoot. Remember, unless you are doing a live shoot in which you are recording directly into the camcorder's audio inputs and that audio is going to serve as the *master* audio in the final music video, you will be using the *studio recording* as the master audio. However, as I discuss in other areas of this book, even a live recording is likely to have audio recorded on a separate recording device, hence the practical need for a clapper once again.

That's Wild

If you've ever heard the expression "recording wild," it does not refer to the personalities of the crew (although in some instances it may—but that's just a coincidence). Recording wild means recording with no clapper for the shot. Shooting wild may be done for several reasons, chief among them is to record audio snippets that can be used later, such as the ambience of a room in a particular scene. Another reason is similar, but with video being the key factor. If you're shooting *B-roll* (footage to which you cut away), there is likely no clapper involved, as synchronization is not a necessity. Here you are essentially shooting wild as well, but for purposes of acquiring additional video footage.

Recording the Audio in a Live Event

As mentioned in Chapter 7, the most straightforward way of recording a live event is to turn on the camcorder at the beginning of a song, keep it running throughout the song until it ends, and use the audio inputs of the camcorder to record the final audio. However, there are two problems with this method. One problem is that a one-take music video tends to be boring; the other problem is that this method doesn't provide you with the best audio quality possible.

First, I'll explain why this method can make for a boring music video; then I'll go into a more detailed explanation about how this approach affects audio quality.

Even if the camera is on a tripod (and it should be), a three-minute, one-shot recording of a song from beginning to end with one camera will resemble a home video more than it will a music video. The audience, just like you, is accustomed to seeing cuts—close-ups, medium shots, and establishing shots. They expect to see shots of the guitarist cutting to the lead singer cutting to the audience cutting to the drummer. They are used to seeing quick cuts, and a one-shot recording might just put them into a coma. Remember, you are already beyond the expectations of the MTV generation.

Audio Quality

The audio quality of a camcorder is not all that bad. It records digital PCM (pulse code modulation) data and thus is a digital recorder. But the camcorder's electronics are devoted to both audio and video, so don't expect to get the same results that you would in a studio recording or with audio gear that has much better A/D and D/A converters, which convert signals from analog to digital and back again. Professional-grade camcorders also use high-quality connectors and cables, something that consumer-grade camcorders do not have. Additionally, many camcorders use just a single IC (integrated circuit) chip to handle the audio chores.

Consumer camcorders also use AGC, which stands for automatic gain control. This feature will average out the overall level so that it doesn't exceed the maximum level before distortion might set in. It is essentially a compressor/limiter that controls your audio levels. This might be beneficial in some instances, but in other cases—such as those in which the main audio (like a speaker) pauses—the background audio (usually noise or ambience) suddenly jumps up in level. Better control and professional results come with using the manual audio controls, coupled with using headphones to check the audio as you are taping.

Some of these differences are minute, and some are more extreme. But remember, you are making a music video; hence, the audio quality is of utmost importance. And that is why you should avoid using the camcorder's internal microphone for recording a live music video. You would not be getting a direct signal this way and could also pick up noise generated by the camcorder's internal motors.

The method you use for recording the audio is ultimately up to you, but here are some choices for recording the live audio (these are illustrated in Figure 8.5):

▷ Recording from the house mixer's stereo outputs directly into the camcorder's audio inputs (number 1 on the figure).

▷ Recording the audio to a separate digital recorder, such as an iPod or iPhone or a DAT machine, while using a clapper or slate (number 2 on the figure).

▷ Recording audio to a separate digital recorder using SMPTE timecode (number 3 on the figure).

▷ Recording audio to a separate digital *multitrack* recorder along with SMPTE timecode. There are apps available for the iPod or iPhone that turn it into a 24-bit, 4-track recorder (number 4 on the figure).

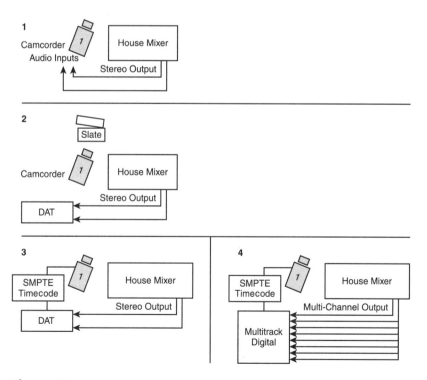

Figure 8.5
Four ways of recording audio during a live shoot.

Option 1, recording from the house mixer directly into the camcorder's audio inputs, is first discussed in Chapter 7. This option means you avoid any synchronization issues (because the audio and video are recorded together and are automatically in sync). It has the disadvantages discussed earlier in this chapter in the section "Audio Quality."

Option 2, recording to a separate digital recorder, can offer better audio quality. This is where a clapper or slate becomes very important, so that you have an exact reference point for syncing up the audio and video tracks later. As in the other options, you ideally want to connect to the stereo output of the house mixer.

Option 3 is available in higher-end equipment in which the same timecode is recorded on both the camcorder and the separate audio recorder. Additional synchronization devices (or add-in hardware cards) are usually necessary to act as an interface between the two machines, with one machine being the "master" and the other machine being a "slave" (*someone* has to be in charge). Again, the stereo audio track could come directly from the house mixer.

Option 4 combines the best of all worlds. Here, you record audio separately along with SMPTE timecode. The difference in this option lies in recording the audio to a *multitrack* recorder instead of a stereo recorder. In this case, you have to think in terms of sub-mixes or "stems." For example, say you have an 8-track multitrack recorder (and no, not the 8-track tape of the seventies!). You have the capability to mix to eight major groupings. An example might look like the one in the following table.

Sub-Mix to Eight Discrete Tracks

Track Number	Description
1	Drums Left
2	Drums Right
3	Bass
4	Lead Guitar
5	Rhythm Guitar
6	Piano
7	Vocals
8	Synthesizer (or timecode if it requires its own track)

These particular channels can be fed from the house mixer output to your setup. The advantage of mixing to separate tracks is that it still gives you the opportunity to make adjustments to these tracks later. The adjustment can certainly imply relative levels, but also can mean equalization, compression, flanging, and other specific effects. The track listing shown in the table is just an example—you can create sub-mixes in any configuration you like. Remember, though, that if you mix to a 2-track master, you no longer have control over these individual elements.

When you watch a concert performance by a major artist, whether you're watching it live or on a DVD presentation, try to take a closer look at the audio setup. It's usually in the middle of the arena, halfway back or more. You will naturally see the huge mixing board. But you also may notice one or more multitrack recorders. This is because almost every major artist will record to multitrack for the opportunity to do post-production on the audio portion of the program as well as the video.

This type of recording needn't be reserved for major artists, however. One inexpensive way to go is to buy a used Tascam D-88 or ADAT or similar digital multitrack (there are also inexpensive hard disk-based systems). These machines used to command a lot of money, but with the evolution of the DAW, the usage of these particular machines has declined greatly, and so has the price.

If you were to have a situation in which a separate company is in charge of audio for the event but you want some independent control of the tracks, you could opt to inject a mixer into your setup. This mixer could also be fed from the house mixer and placed before your digital multitrack, but you could elect to be "fed" different sub-mixes, as you would also have control over the individual levels.

The Live, Multi-Camera Shoot

As the name implies, a multi-camera shoot uses more than one camera. It may mean using two, three, four, or more cameras—but regardless of the number, the idea is to have multiple angles recorded—in sync—so that multiple shots are created simultaneously (see Figure 8.6). You could have one or more cameras shooting wild, but if you want to save money on aspirin or other pain relievers, shooting as much as possible in sync is the way to go.

The multi-camera shoot originated a long time ago with situation comedies that were taped this way. As a matter of fact, if you wanted to, you could add a few pieces of gear and shoot your event as if it were a television show, saving a lot of time in your post-production editing.

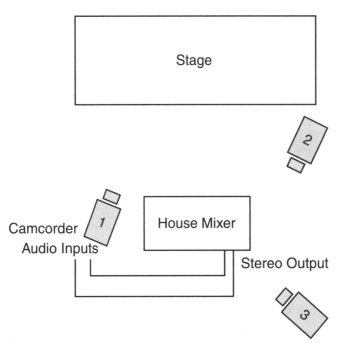

Figure 8.6
An example of how multiple cameras might be positioned in a live shoot of a performance.

If the multiple cameras are fed to a switcher—a sort of "mixer" for video sources (as opposed to just audio sources), the output of the switcher can reflect the various takes that you (as the director) are calling for. You may have seen this portrayed in a movie or on television. The director is in the control room shouting out commands such as those shown in the following table.

Each camera is previewed on its own monitor while a "program monitor" reflects the current image that is being taken—meaning, the image that is going to tape or broadcast antenna or satellite (see Figure 8.7). That's the interesting thing about this kind of setup— it can be a situation that is a live broadcast, or it can be a scenario in which the entire feed is simply recorded for a later purpose. This situation also allows for additional editing if necessary.

Example Verbal Direction in a Multi-Camera Shoot

Command	Meaning
"Ready one—take one"	Technical director (TD) presses a button or slider, choosing camera one on the switcher.
"Ready two"	Cameraman two has a good shot framed and holds it there.
"Take two"	The TD brings up camera two on the switcher.
"Okay, three pan left and frame the vocalist in a CU"	Cameraman three pans left and lines up a shot in which the vocalist is front and center in a close-up.
"Ready three"	Cameraman three holds his shot, and the TD gets ready to bring it up.
"One—give me a wide shot of the stage—Take three"	The TD presses the button or slider to bring up camera three while cameraman one zooms out to get a wide shot of the stage.

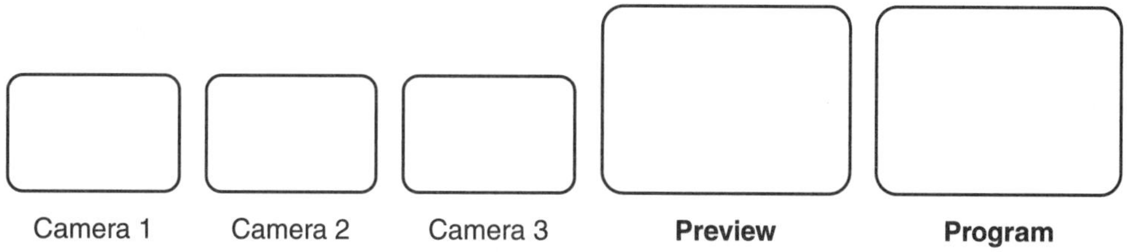

Camera 1   Camera 2   Camera 3   **Preview**   **Program**

Figure 8.7
A typical setup for a live shoot includes monitors for each camera, a preview monitor (the camera that's cued up), and a program monitor.

In the case of a music video, you would probably not treat it as a live broadcast as you would be locked into whatever decisions you made during the event. You could, however, use a combination of ideas in which you treat it as a live event but also ensure that each of the individual camera shots is taped. This is a great advantage of today's camcorders. You can feed an external source (such as a switcher) but also record everything on a teeny-tiny tape or disc or hard drive. When you think of the huge, bulky television cameras of yesteryear, you can see that we've come a long way.

Another thing to keep in mind is that if you do decide to integrate other footage later in post-production, you can still do that—even if you started out thinking that a simple live shoot of a concert or band performance is all you need. With multiple cameras and a line cut (that's the scenario I've described using a switcher), you've saved some time in the editing room. With each camera recording its own footage, you have other creative choices that you can make later. All of this can ultimately be intercut with any ideas you have later—ideas that were not necessarily filmed at the live event.

Multiple Takes on Tape

Shooting your music video with no intention of creating a live event is almost the other extreme, at least in terms of time. In a live taping, you are making instantaneous decisions and relying on the talent—both of the performer and the crew—to be experienced enough to get things right the first time. If you're taping solely for a post-production scenario, people very often don't get it right the first, second, third, or fourth time (or more). That's why a director in this situation is often heard to say, "Okay, just one more," meaning one more take.

On the other hand, you will have many more shots to choose from, and you'll have the ability to "sculpt" the final product to your liking in post-production. In a live shoot, you might have to settle for whatever you get. In a taping, you don't have to settle until you're convinced you've captured the best possible shot that can be made.

The reference to a director saying "Okay, just one more" can be the basis of skepticism about the film business and a suspicion of possible self-indulgence on the part of filmmakers (when there are dozens and dozens of takes), but the truth is that there's a lot to be gained by getting "just the right take." It can be costly and sometimes impossible to reshoot a particular scene later, for you'd have to create precisely the same conditions that you originally had. This would apply to getting the right angle on a shot of the band, but could apply even more to a scene that involves actors or band members playing a role in a particular scene. As a director, you must have an awareness that is both extremely focused yet broad enough to take all things into consideration.

For example, if you have a creative shot in which lighting plays a key role and you have a great dolly-in shot planned, you could very well find out later that the actor underperformed when saying his or her lines. Your focus might have been on the creative aspects of the scene but at the expense of having convincing dialogue. That's why it's a matter of having intense focus and broad awareness at the same time.

Multiple takes are common in filmmaking, and if necessary, you should not hesitate to use them in your music video production. You don't want to wear out your talent, but at the same time, you want to ensure you've captured exactly what you need. And the opposite is sometimes true—that you capture precisely what you want on the first take and that it even exceeds your expectations. You could very well find that subsequent takes don't even come close to the spontaneity or spark that the first take had. It's your job to know which is which.

Another reason for doing multiple takes may have nothing to do with whether the shot was good or bad, but incorporates the idea of a multi-camera shoot. Unless you're planning to employ a pyrotechnics team to create special effects, such as blowing up a building, you're unlikely to need a multi-camera setup. With a single camera shoot, you can shoot the same scene, multiple times, from different angles. If you create a storyboard, then you already know what these different shots are going to look like. If you don't have a story-board, you can still use your creativity while on location to capture different camera angles for a particular scene. Nevertheless, the principles just stated for doing multiple takes for one camera angle—but ensuring you get a usable take—still apply. Thus, you need to think in terms of getting a good take for each of multiple angles.

A third example of employing multiple takes is capturing footage for the same scene but with a different bent. For example, say your music video calls for a scene in which the female lead singer lip syncs the words "I love you" as she looks straight into the eyes of the actor playing her love interest. That's fine, but what if you discover in post-production that the scene would be more effective if she were looking straight into the camera? Right now, you're not totally certain which shot will work best as you can argue advantages and disadvantages to both ideas. The smart director will shoot both versions (using multiple takes of each, if necessary) and thank himself when it comes time for post-production and both options are still available. The trick (even for a smart director) is knowing ahead of time that different versions of the same scene will be valuable later and being ready to shoot them when the time comes.

And finally, a fourth reason for multiple takes is capturing footage for a section of the song—for example, a verse, chorus, or bridge—that will be used a second or third time later in the song. You might argue that these are not multiple takes, but rather different scenes altogether. I believe both viewpoints are correct, but the advantage in looking at them as different takes will be a benefit in the pre-production stage—namely, planning how the same chorus could be shot in different ways (subtlety or not) to keep the interest going.

The moral to this story is you need to have lots of tape (or hard disk space, or whatever storage device your camcorder uses) to create your project. A good rule of thumb is that you'll probably need more storage than you think you'll ever use, so get it and bring it with you. Figure 8.8 shows both CD and tape storage media, but this photo could easily have hard disks and flash drives added to the pile.

Figure 8.8
Tape, CD, hard drive—no matter what your storage medium,
plan to have plenty of it (more than you think you'll need).

Multiple Locations

Shooting scenes multiple times obviously has its advantages, but shooting scenes in *multiple locations* for the same section of a song provides additional benefits. I call it out separately here because it's a very simple concept for a music video, and you've likely seen it used many times. For example, in verse one, the band might be filmed singing in the studio, but in verse two, the shot is framed exactly the same way but is taped in an outside location with a beautiful panoramic landscape in the background. Verse three might also be shot in a different location or in the same location as verse one.

This technique can be used in either a literal or abstract way. If the lyrics in verse two were somehow related to the outdoors or countryside, the location would be a literal representation of that idea. If there were no relationship at all, the use of a different location would still work. This type of artistic license was popularized a long time ago with the earliest of the MTV generation of music videos. No explanation of the scene change is necessary. The use of the scene change simply is—for the lack of a better word—cool.

Camera Moves and Camera Angles

Camera moves and camera angles add another method of creating diverse scenes. Some of these moves can be subtle and some much more dramatic. Having an understanding of what you can accomplish with camera moves and camera angles can help you spice up your video, and in most cases, you will not need a larger budget to create them.

Camera Moves

The most basic method of shooting anything is the handheld shot—simply pick up the camera and let it roll. This may not be the best way to get a smooth, steady shot—but in fact, an unsteady, somewhat bumpy shot may be the effect you're looking for. Capturing this type of footage is common in "contemporary" film and video projects, including the music video.

The next most basic thing is mounting the camera on a tripod. This provides a means to get a variety of camera angles (which I'm about to discuss) with a certain amount of precision.

Music videos with larger budgets often employ the use of cranes to add more impact to this idea. The different shots might vary dramatically in the type of camera movement that is used, with the crane adding lots of drama by doing flyovers or lifts that add a completely different perspective to the way the scene started out.

Another camera move that adds drama is the dolly shot. A dolly can be a platform or a cart on wheels that serves as the foundation for the camera and tripod. The dolly shot follows the action. For example, two characters in a movie might be having a conversation as they walk down the street, but instead of panning as they walk by, the dolly shot moves right along with them. The key to a good dolly shot is that it is very smooth, unlike a handheld shot that might also be used to follow two characters. Major motion pictures will often use a dolly that runs on two tracks that have been laid down—another way of ensuring that the shot is super smooth. You can see the dolly shot compared to the pan shot in Figure 8.9.

There is another way to achieve smoothness without using a dolly. The Steadicam, invented in 1976, is a device that straps onto the cameraman, and by virtue of some neat technology, including gimbals and gyroscopes, the cameraman can walk through (or around or next to) an actor or object without creating any bumpiness. The Steadicam is truly steady, and like other camera equipment, can be bought or rented for a production. Having said that, I would recommend hiring a Steadicam operator if you plan to use one in your production. It requires a lot of skill and practice to master it effectively.

Figure 8.9
In a pan shot (left), the camera is stationary on a tripod, whereas a dolly shot (right) follows the action regardless of the direction the subject is moving.

Your vision for your music video should dictate what you need in terms of extra camera equipment, and naturally this will be tempered by the realities of your budget. But always keep in mind that great things can be achieved by being inventive and resourceful. Dollies and cranes are great if you can afford them, but in fact you may need a grainy, bumpy filming approach for your particular project—or you may be able to come up with inventive ways of creating the *effect* of dollies or cranes without having to rent them.

Camera Angles

Shots that do not necessitate sophisticated gear certainly will save you money, but this does not imply that they are insignificant in their impact. The trick is knowing what effect a certain type of shot will have on the message you are communicating.

Pan shots are horizontal moves that can be done handheld or on a tripod, although if smoothness is the desired result, a tripod is the right choice. Pan shots also follow the action, but the camera is in the same spot from the beginning to the end of the shot. The pan shot pivots from a central point and moves—say from left to right—while in the dolly shot, the camera does not stay in the same spot at all. If you are using a pan shot to film two people walking down the street, you need to provide some space in front of the characters as they walk. In a sense, the camera should lead them with this extra space. You may notice this same method employed in still photography. If the subject is a person looking slightly to the right, there is more "blank area" on the right side of the picture. You can see this illustrated in Figure 8.10. It is framed that way on purpose, and when it is not done that way, it can actually make the viewer feel somewhat uncomfortable. Knowing this rule, you can then break it to achieve the opposite effect. If you have the leading space behind the characters in a scary scene, you might be implying that the "monster" is sneaking up behind them. Make sure there's a purpose to the way in which you frame the scene.

Figure 8.10
Whether in still photos or motion video, you should provide a leading space in the direction the subject is looking or moving, shown here on the right side of the image.

The *tilt shot* is like the pan shot except it goes in a vertical pattern, up and down. The tilt, like the pan, can also be done with a handheld camcorder or on a tripod—with the same rules regarding how smooth a shot you want to capture. Think of a tennis player serving the ball, with the camera shot following the ball as it's lifted straight up into the air. If the scene called for capturing just that particular part of the move, you would be using a tilt shot.

The *tilted angle shot* (as opposed to the tilt shot) is made by tilting the camera to one side or the other at an angle, for example, at 45 degrees. This is often used to create imbalance, uncertainty, or fear. It harkens back to the days of Alfred Hitchcock and has been used many times in suspense, horror, and science fiction movies. The key is to use it when it is warranted, not just for the sake of offering up a new camera angle. If you ever watched the original episodes of *The Twilight Zone,* you saw it used there as well; although when used effectively, most viewers are not even aware that a tilt shot is used.

High angle shots, in which the camera points down on the subject, usually create the illusion that the subject is less important or insignificant. *Low angle shots* shoot upward and add importance or power to the subject. Like the other shots discussed, use high angle and low angle shots only when the scene calls for them—not just for the sake of changing the camera's perspective.

Costume Changes

Another effect you've probably seen before in music videos is not very hard to duplicate. Instead of varying the camera shot or location, you can insert a new variable into the mix— a costume change. Although a costume change makes sense when it coincides with a scene change in a motion picture or play, having the artist use a costume change simply because you're filming the chorus section a second time in a music video does not really make sense. But that doesn't matter. Again, it's creative license, and it adds more variety to the video. The fact that it does *not* make sense has a slightly jarring effect. But no one will stop watching because of this—quite the opposite is true, as it tends to spice things up and maintain interest.

Although you will find more about them in Chapter 9, "Post-Production", because they are sometimes related to the subject of artistic license, I will mention the match cut and jump cut here.

The *match cut* is an edit in which the scene that you cut to is framed like and almost identical to the scene before it. Think of a scene in which a shot of the moon is featured, dead center in the frame. The scene then dissolves or cuts to an image of a clock. The clock is precisely (or close to) the size of the moon in the previous shot. Although this is not hugely difficult to achieve from a technical perspective, it nevertheless can have a dramatic effect on the transition between these two scenes.

In a *jump cut*, on the other hand, the editor has no intention of trying to make the first and second scenes match. Think of unedited footage in which you are filming some action, then you stop the camera, and moments later resume shooting without changing the framing of the shot. The image "jumps" rather suddenly from the first shot to the second shot. In "days of old," a jump cut was looked upon as poor editing. Today, it is used intentionally as an effect and is regarded as cool (when used sparingly).

Now, the reason I bring this up in the context of costume changes is that both the match cut and jump cut are often used to create instant "magical" costume changes onscreen. A match cut is more difficult to achieve, as the subject must be in exactly the same physical place, with a similar facial expression, and framed exactly the same way. If you can pull it off, however, a match cut can be very effective.

But a jump cut works very well in this situation because we know (subconsciously, at least) that a band cannot perform a complete costume change in one millisecond. Thus, the jarring effect of a jump cut fits well with a transition that is really impossible (in real life) in the first place. To the viewer, it is unlikely that any of this is being considered for even a moment; nevertheless, the viewer accepts the jump cut, when used this way, as perfectly normal.

To the larger question of why to do a costume change at all with either a match cut or jump cut, the answer is, no particular reason. But if the effect works and doesn't seem obligatory, you might consider it. The role of the artist is to have a change of clothing for this scene. The role of the director is to stage the scene well so that the match or jump cut is relatively easy to pull off during the editing process.

Shooting B-Roll

Shooting B-roll has nothing to do with B-movies. B-roll is simply footage that you can cut away.

Earlier in this chapter in the section "That's Wild," B-roll was mentioned in the context of synchronization and the fact that you aren't likely to need a clapper at the beginning of every scene. Now I will take another look at what B-roll footage might include.

The following scenario presents a typical example of B-roll shooting. An executive from a company is being interviewed on camera about his company's financial success the preceding year. After 20 or 30 seconds of talking, the video cuts to an outside shot of the building as the executive continues to talk. This cut is followed by a close-up of the signage outside showing the company name and logo. Finally, the video cuts back to the executive speaking on camera.

Naturally, this was not how the sequence was shot that day. The interview took place entirely with the executive being on camera. The other footage of the building was probably shot the same day, but at a different time. It's quite possible that the director did not know for certain whether that particular footage would be used. However, the director usually has a general idea about the kinds of shots he might use later during the editing process. He was smart—he shot some B-roll.

You should keep B-roll shooting in mind, even if it's not specifically indicated in your script. Ideas for shooting B-roll sometimes come to mind when you're on the scene. One of the worst feelings in the world is to be in the editing process and realize something like, "I should have taken a shot of the ocean...we were right there, and we didn't take a wide shot of the ocean!"

Making a Scene—Terminology

Clarification of terminology is relevant, especially because some of the terms related to a scene are used interchangeably, even though they refer to different concepts. So, for the record, keep these definitions in mind:

> ▷ **Scene:** A scene refers to a specific location. All the shots discussed in this section on shooting live make up a scene. If you leave the location on the beach and shoot more footage in front of an office building, you have changed scenes.

> ▷ **Setup:** A setup is a shot (or series of shots) taken from one specific camera angle. There may be several setups that constitute one scene. Different types of shots (such as close-up, wide, medium) are also identified as different setups.

> ▷ **Take:** A take refers to the repetitive shots that are taken of a particular scene until the director (that's you) feels it's as perfect as possible.

There may be multiple takes and multiple setups that comprise a scene, and multiple scenes are what make up your entire video production.

Do's and Don'ts (Especially the Don'ts)

If you are an experienced filmmaker, some of the following will seem very basic to you. But because this book is targeted to a wide variety of readers with different skill sets, I'm going to mention a few basic do's and don'ts that might prove valuable and be a time saver as well.

First, because it's a longer list, here are the don'ts.

> ▷ Don't use the camera's titling feature. You will create the titles in post-production, where you not only have better control, but also a much more professional look to your fonts, as well as a variety of methods to display the titles.

> ▷ Don't use the camera's special effects features. The preceding rules also apply here.

> ▷ Don't take your collection of cables, adaptors, batteries, filters, and so on to the set without organizing them carefully in a camera bag.

▷ Don't forget your camera bag.

▷ Don't assume that a bad shot (as a result of such things as poor lighting, excessive camera movement, and so on) can be fixed later in post-production. Get the best possible shots you can during the live shoot.

▷ Don't proceed with your production if you're using outside actors without first getting releases.

▷ Don't view your production as an amateur one. If you look at it that way, so will everyone else. Go to the set feeling like a pro (except, perhaps, for the oversized ego).

Now, for the Do's.

▷ Use a variety of checklists to ensure everything is complete. You might have one for tools to bring, another for things to do, and another checklist that is an actual shot list.

▷ Make a shooting schedule. This is a project plan that details where and when scenes are to be shot, which resources (including the artist and/or other actors) are needed for that day, and so on.

▷ Make a call sheet. This is for the cast and crew and is a document stating where and when scenes are to be shot, contact information for those involved, a schedule for that particular day, the location, and so on.

▷ Use a video monitor on-site. This is for the purposes of shooting and playing back video. A video monitor that's hooked up to the output of the camera(s) is a more reliable means of viewing footage than the two- or three-inch LCD monitor on the camera. Additionally, it provides a means for several people on the set to see the footage at one time.

▷ Use headphones to monitor audio while shooting, and if the external monitor doesn't have its own speakers, bring a pair of small speakers (preferably, powered speakers) to the set as well.

Logging and Staying Organized

Have you ever been accused of being *too* organized? Have people said things to you like, "you're so methodical" or "you're so detail-oriented" or even "you're so anal-retentive"? If so, this is your lucky day, because these qualities are a part of what is necessary to successfully create a video production. If you don't have these qualities, you've got some work to do— that is, unless you can afford to hire a production assistant or script supervisor who is more organized than you are.

During the Shoot

It is important that each scene, setup, and take in your production is logged in a log book. Some people prefer to do this during the actual shoot. However, it is also possible to do this at the end of the day or the following morning. Hollywood productions refer to this as watching the "dailies." This gives the key personnel a chance to review footage, and it also provides an opportunity to log each of the scenes.

The Log Sheet

A log sheet can be very detailed or very simple. At the least, it should contain the tape number, information on which scene is being shot, the date, the location, the start time, the end time, and any other additional notes that describe the shots. You can make up a bunch of blank log sheets and put them in a binder, or you can search on the Internet for some ready-made log sheets—some of which are free of charge. (You might search on a topic using the keywords "log sheets film video".)

The detail included on a log sheet is directly proportional to the complexity of your project. For example, with a multi-camera shoot, you might include A, B, or C, each letter representing a different camera. You will be very happy later in the editing room if you also included the specific setup and type of shot, such as CU for close-up, WS for wide shot, MS for medium shot, and so on. When there are multiple takes, it is important to include the take numbers—and in the description, you can denote if a particular take is good or bad. (You could indicate NG for "no good.") For the start and ending times, you can include the timecode. If you can indicate the timecode specifically down to the frame, such as 01.29.58.06, that's fine, but even a more general one can suffice for the initial logging during a shoot, whereas a specific timecode can be derived later when reviewing dailies.

It is a good idea to start a new page whenever you start a new tape or reel. A new reel deserves a new page and makes your job easier later when sorting through all the tapes.

Labeling Tapes

You won't have any luck keeping accurate logs if you don't label your tapes. Just as with the log, it's good practice to have a fresh tape correspond to a new reel.

Perhaps you are the kind of person who doesn't label tapes because you

> ▷ Don't have time for that.

> ▷ Know in your head what's on each reel.

> ▷ Can't bother with inconsequential details.

> ▷ Will figure it out later.

If this is the case, you had better start getting in the habit of tape labeling. None of these excuses will work in a professional scenario—as a matter of fact, the habit of not labeling tapes doesn't work well with simple home movies. You will probably want to come up with some sort of system for tape labeling that works well for you. In all cases, you will want to include the date. Other codes might be M, indicating a master tape; S might stand for a source tape; C might be a compilation tape; and so on. On a specific project, such as your music video, R and a corresponding number could stand for reel number. None of this is set in stone—you can come up with a system that works for you. The only thing set in stone is that it's a bad idea *not* to label tapes—that is, once again—unless you have a full-time production assistant to do these types of chores for you.

After the Shoot

After the shoot, gather all of the source tapes and organize them by reel number (which should be easy because you are an experienced tape labeler). Keep them together in one place or, better yet, one container (such as a box) that you keep in one place.

Although it's not an absolute necessity to enter your log sheet information into a computer, there are some benefits to doing so. If you use a program such as Microsoft Excel to keep track of the logging information, you can easily sort through your information by date, reel number, timecode, content, and so on. Most schedules are tight; therefore, it is understandable if there is no time to enter this data into a computer. But, if time allows, this method can help you out in the long run.

Keep your tapes in a cool, dry place, and out of direct sunlight. Keep them away from magnetic fields (which sometimes can be generated from a television set or speakers). Treat them with care, because they are both your source tapes and your archival tapes.

You should also lock your tapes by flipping the little switch on the top of the MiniDV cassette. There's nothing worse than telling the boss (even if *you're* the boss) that the opening shots were recorded over when you taped your sister's baby shower, forgetting that Reel 1 was still in the camcorder.

By now, you can surmise that these basic housekeeping duties are vital for a successful production. It's true that a production can be completed without the details being tracked and organized. However, these details can be like a box of disorganized cables—even though they're all there, if they're disorganized, you'll only be adding to your own confusion unless some sort of organization and methodology are in place.

Special Considerations for Shooting a Music Video

Here are some principles to keep in mind when shooting your music video:

▷ Music videos tend to have more visual effects, extreme camera movements, jump cuts, and so on than do "normal" videos. Feel free to use such effects and techniques, but do not *overuse* them just because they're cool. Use effects when they make sense.

▷ You don't shoot a video and then consider the role of the music. The opposite is the case (which is different than almost all other video productions). The music is the heart of the video, and the video serves the music.

▷ A lot of your editing will involve cutting to the beat (more about this in Chapter 9). Keep the rhythm of the video aligned with that of the music. Keep this rhythm in mind when you are shooting your footage.

▷ Be original. This is a tough one, because almost every music video is derivative in some way, copying or leveraging what's been done in other music videos. To be truly original (while maintaining viewer interest) is not an easy task, but if you can do it, you will be the one who everyone else begins to imitate later. (Consider it a compliment.)

▷ Have fun. Producing a music video is a lot of work, but it should be fun as well. If it isn't fun, consider producing nature videos, aerobics videos, or infomercials. (Chances are, however, that those will be much *less* fun.)

With the pre-production and shoot completed, it's time to move on Chapter 9. This really *is* the fun part of the process, when all the pieces begin to fall together and your vision for your music video takes shape.

Post-Production

SOMETIMES THE TERMS POST-PRODUCTION and editing are used interchangeably, although in practice, editing is best viewed as a part of the overall post-production process. You can think of post-production as everything that takes place from the time shooting is completed to the creation of the final master.

Just as with other chapters in this book, this chapter is not intended to give you a complete and in-depth understanding of the editing process. The focus is on the basic parts of the editing process and especially the parts that are important when creating a music video.

Editing Considerations

If you are into creating music, and I'm going to make a huge leap and assume that you are, then you know that being a musician is part art and part science. Art is the creative part of the formula while science might be represented by technique. Many professions have this part science/part art composition. A ballet dancer, a marketing director, and a car salesman all have this mix to one degree or another.

Film and video editors are another group that has this hybrid make-up. When you take a close-up look at the editing process, you might be looking at the nits and technicalities of SMPTE timecode. (Don't worry; you'll read about that in a moment.) You could, in the same discussion, be focused on the topic of artistic license—how to break away from the norm, experiment, and explore unchartered creative territory. Editing is part art and part science, too.

This chapter covers SMPTE timecode and artistic license, as well as other topics that are a part of the art and science of editing. The focus is on editing music videos and the chapter includes some of the things to look for in a video editing software package.

Art and Science

Editing, in its most basic form, involves removing the bad shots and leaving the good ones. Sometimes this is an obvious procedure, such as those instances in which you didn't know the camera was still running and you ended up with a shaky, out-of-focus medium shot of your feet walking along the sidewalk. That shot will be removed in its entirety, and it doesn't take a lot of thought to come to that conclusion.

The other part of editing is more of a challenge. What you want to accomplish by editing is the sequencing of the good shots to create something that is interesting, compelling, and possibly emotionally moving—and at the very least, a series of images and sounds that tells a story.

The science—or craft—of editing involves the use of editing software, syncing with SMPTE timecode (see Figure 9.1 and the upcoming sidebar, "What Is SMPTE," for more on time-codes), and a basic understanding of editing concepts such as rippling, inserts, trimming, overwriting, and so forth. (See more on these topics in the section " Inserting, Trimming, Rippling, and Overwriting," later in this chapter.)

01:01:42:21.15

Figure 9.1
SMPTE (Society of Motion Picture and Television Engineers) timecode
can be displayed in hours, minutes, seconds, frames, and samples.

What Is SMPTE?

Technically, SMPTE is an acronym for an organization known as the Society of
Motion Picture and Television Engineers. The common usage of the term refers
to the *timecode standard* that the society developed, which describes time in terms
of hours, minutes, seconds, frames, and samples. This standard is used in film and
video production, as well as computer-based music production.

Years ago, it was necessary to manually "stripe" audio and/or video tracks with
SMPTE timecode as a method of syncing everything up later. Today, SMPTE is
automatically striped on just about everything to do with film, video, and audio
production.

Even your common camcorder is likely to have SMPTE recorded along with the
picture and sound. Your editing process will benefit greatly by referring to timecode,
especially when you use B-roll or cutaway shots. SMPTE is the timing standard that
keeps everything in sync.

The art of editing can be learned only to a point, whether by instruction or reading a book
on the subject. Like other art forms, its effectiveness depends largely on the artist.

For example, go back to the bad stuff I suggested removing from a shot. Removing the bad
footage is a no-brainer. But if you are left, say, with a shot of a street scene and want to cut
to a close-up of one of the shops on that street, where—exactly—do you cut from one scene
to the next? Removing the bad footage is not enough. There is a certain rhythm created by
both the camera motion and the length of the shots that comes before and after these two
scenes. The pacing of the video sequence is related to the length of the shots. The precise
editing points are dictated by what is happening at a given moment in the frame.

When you start editing, you get a feel for where one shot should end and where the next one should begin. Perhaps the street shot is wide—panning from left to right and stopping at the store you're going to cut to. The store may be a medium shot that tilts up from the doorway to the sign above the store, where it stops and holds just long enough for the viewer to absorb the store's name (see Figure 9.2).

Figure 9.2
The editing process has a logical flow and a rhythm built into it.
A street scene might pan and cut to a store sign, which would then cut to the inside of the store.

If some of this seems obvious to you, that's a good thing. Hopefully, you have a natural inclination as to where to make edits that flow and create a rhythm of their own. Some of this is very intuitive and gets better with practice. Knowing this and understanding that there is an art to editing that goes beyond the basics, you need to be constantly aware as to exactly where and when you make your edit points. The final product will be the sum of those decisions.

And because I'm talking about art—especially because this discussion focuses on music videos—you want the final product to be more than a series of shots, one after the other. Remember, the medium is the message—so this is your chance to use the medium in an artful way.

DIY or Not?

The decision whether to perform the editing yourself, as opposed to hiring someone else, goes back to a discussion in Chapter 4, "Choosing Your Production Methods," that demonstrated DIY decisions are directly related to budget. If you're producing a video that provides for a budget to hire a professional editor, then this is something to consider. One of the advantages to using a professional, besides the fact that this editor can produce very professional-looking results, is that he sees the project with a pair of fresh eyes, much in the same way that a hired producer/engineer might bring something more to your final mix than you could (by being so close to it).

On the other hand, lower budgets can still result in professional quality as you literally learn on the job. The learning will involve both the art and science of editing. You will need to understand the editing process; that's for certain. You will need to learn about your editing software to the extent that you can create just about anything you can envision. And, once again, to create a product that is more than the sum of its parts, you will need to be artful in your approach to editing. If you are passionate enough about doing so, there really is nothing to stop you.

Editing for a Music Video

The basic principles that apply to video editing apply to music videos as well. Where it differs has everything to do with the music—the music is paramount and "in charge" of everything else. Music is the driver; video is the vehicle. The following sections cover some of the basics and naturally, the topics that are specific to editing music videos.

The Beat Goes On

So, for the sake of argument, say that you've already mastered the art and science of editing. How then is a music video different from any other type of video when it comes to the editing process?

As discussed earlier, it is the music that is driving the video. Now that you are editing, you will soon discover that it's the *beat* that drives the *music* that drives the *video*.

Cutting to the beat has been an editing method that goes back to the very first music videos. Consider this typical example of music: A rock piece in 4/4 time that consists of drums, bass, guitar, piano, and vocals can be edited to the kick drum. Depending on the pacing you want to achieve, the cuts may fall on every other measure, or every measure, or twice or even four times a measure (see Figures 9.3 and 9.4). Most likely, you will mix it all up and create a visual rhythm that varies within the song structure. In other words, it doesn't require that you cut only to every measure—you can combine any number of editing points dictated by a variety of beats.

Figure 9.3
The vertical lines in this Final Cut example indicate which places in the audio's waveform are likely possibilities for making a visual edit.

A simple example is an editing rhythm that falls on every measure, but when the song comes to a drum fill, the video cuts on each part of the tom fill, which could be eighth or sixteenth notes. Then, as the next downbeat begins, you return to the previous pacing and cutting method on each measure. I'm simplifying here so that the point is clear. In reality, you can mix it up even more to make the final edit more compelling.

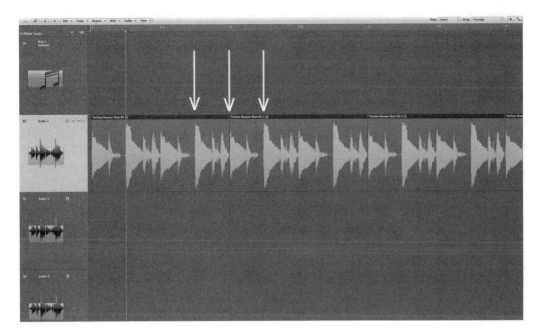

Figure 9.4
This is an audio waveform—closer up—showing places where you might cut to the beat.

A ballad might have a different rhythm altogether. The pace will be slower, just as the tempo is slower in a ballad. The cuts don't necessarily have to land on a beat. As a matter of fact, there is no law that cuts have to land on a beat, even in the first example of a faster rock tune. You may cut this way—or you may not.

Learn the rules. Once you feel you have them down well, break a few. It's all about you and your creativity.

Artistic License

Another general rule that applies to music videos is that you have much more freedom to experiment, try new ideas, and break away from some of the formal editing rules found in traditional video editing.

One example of how a rule was broken a long time ago is the jump cut. Traditional editing practices taught us never to cut from one part of a scene to another part of the scene, say, a few seconds later—while the camera angle and framing remains the same. The video seems to jump with a jarring movement that is somewhat unnatural and certainly not smooth.

Think of a situation in which an onscreen talking head is speaking and then the video cuts to a sentence that takes place a few seconds later. The person's position, expression, and so on will not match exactly, and thus the cut seems abrupt and unnatural. This is the nature of a jump cut. The sequence shown in Figure 9.5 makes sense as a series of stills, but if the stills represented actual frames in a video sequence, they would be jump cuts. The facial expressions would change suddenly and the people in the background would be jumping around unnaturally.

Figure 9.5
These still shots would be jump cuts if they were contiguous frames of a video sequence.

If you look at the films, television shows, and commercials of today, you will see that the jump cut is used without hesitation. It is used for effect. It is sometimes used, for lack of a better word, as a "hip" way of editing a particular scene. Although you'd hope there is some reason or meaning attached to the use of the jump cut, sometimes there is and sometimes there isn't. But the old rule about not using a jump cut has been broken. The "wrong way" has given way to a new way. The jump cut and other unconventional edits have evolved from being considered "wrong" to being looked at as "cool." Usually, though not always, you will find these new rules employed in videos that are more artistic in nature—such as a music video.

When you edit music videos, you have more artistic license than you have with a documentary or corporate video. But if you do try something new and different, bounce it off a couple of other people before you run with it. Objectivity can be a difficult thing when you are too close to your work for a long period of time. Artistic license can yield great results sometimes. At other times, the results might seem gratuitous, self-indulgent, or downright silly. Luckily, the digital age affords you the opportunity to experiment with new ideas with the assurance that the original digital video files are still there—safe and sound until you want to try something different or revert to an edit that is more traditional in nature.

Before You Cut

You may have heard the saying "We'll fix it in the mix." Even before they had the advantages of digital recording equipment, producers and musicians often skipped the process of redoing or fixing something during recording session, figuring that they would fix it later.

This worked sometimes. Most times, it did not. "We'll fix it in the mix" became a sort of code for "We don't have time to deal with it now, maybe we can do something about it later." This idea also exists in the film and video world with a slight variation: "We'll fix it in post."

Well, now you're in post, so let me throw out a sort of rhetorical question: Did either of these preceding ideas occur during the recording or filming process? I hope the answer is no. Because editing is much more than the process of snipping off the bad footage, you will have plenty to do without worrying how to stabilize a shaky shot or turn day into night. Okay, those are bad examples because they *can* be done in post. But you do want to have well lit scenes, well recorded audio, and a suitable variety of takes to do a good editing job. If you've watched and logged all of your video, you probably have a good idea already of the task ahead. Before you start cutting, try to identify any real problem areas that might exist and determine what you need to do to correct them. If something must be reshot, you can get those wheels in motion while you begin your editing process.

Editing Basics

No matter what kind of video you are producing, there are some standard editing principles that are relevant. If you don't know what they are, you can easily get up to speed by taking advantage of classes or books on the subject. If this is your first time doing any editing, you might want to practice on some footage other than your music video until you get your "editing chops" up.

Editing is really the process of assembling your shots in a cohesive order to make a rough cut. Then you fine-tune it and create a fine cut (and, eventually, a final cut).

Importing Your Footage

Assuming you already have your video-editing software (and if you don't, see the section, "Editing Software," later in this chapter), your first order of business is to *import* the video footage. Hook up your camera to your computer and follow the instructions for importing video. Luckily, most software editing programs are very straightforward and even capable of separating the scenes into individual clips. The importing process is also known as *capturing* in some programs (see Figure 9.6).

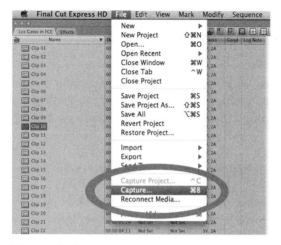

Figure 9.6
The first thing you do in preparation for editing is to import or "capture" your video footage.

Using the Timeline

Most editing programs are based on a *timeline.* You use the timeline to drag and drop clips into the sequence you want. The timeline usually starts at 0 (zero) and, as you add each clip, the video lengthens by the amount of time it takes up. (I say usually starts at 0 because many filmmakers will start at 01:00:00:00, wherein the 01, instead of meaning one hour, means *reel* one.) There is a vertical line that moves from left to right that is similar to a playhead—wherever the playhead is located, that's the exact frame of video you will see. In Figure 9.7, the semicircle surrounds the timeline.

Because you are making a music video, the *assembly* mode of editing (adding clip by clip) is slightly different. Instead of adding clip by clip and thereby adding time, your time is predetermined by your music track. Again, the music drives the video. So, in addition to importing your video into your project, you need to import your song (your master recording) and place it on a stereo audio track—usually a second stereo audio track (see Figure 9.8). In reality, the source audio (which was recorded with the original video) is rarely used. An exception to this might be a segment at the beginning or end of the piece in which possibly some dialogue takes place. But most times, you will not be listening to your source audio. It's the music that tells the story.

Figure 9.7
The timeline is the heart of the editing program, where you assemble clips, audio bits, titles, transitions, and effects to create a rough and/or final cut.

Figure 9.8
You will likely want to place your music on a second stereo audio track, keeping the source audio on the first track in case you want to use it.

Inserting, Trimming, Rippling, and Overwriting

You are usually able to *trim* the clips on the timeline. Trimming can mean either making the clips shorter or making them longer. You will also be doing *insert* editing, in which a clip is added to the timeline. The clip may be inserted anywhere—before, after, or in between existing clips. One type of insert edit will force the existing clips (to the right of the insert) to move to the right by the same amount of time the new clips requires. This is called *rippling*—the net effect of the edit doesn't change the content; it only changes the time at which subsequent clips occur.

There will be many occasions in which you will want to do an *overwrite* edit. An overwrite edit replaces the existing clip by the amount of time the new clip requires. It doesn't push the remaining clips. The timing stays the same; it's the content that changes. Overwriting is often used to cut away to completely different footage that illustrates a different scene, such as what an interviewee (just for example) might be talking about on camera.

Because you are creating a music video, the timing of events is determined by the music. One way to approach the editing process is to insert your clips into the timeline to get a rough cut—an approximation of what visuals you want and in what sequence they will occur. Then you might trim the clips to correspond to the timing of the music. Finally, you might get creative by doing some overwrite edits that replace some of the shots completely, but without changing everything else you've edited up to that point. Then you will likely do some fine-tuning to get the edits as precise as possible.

The Music Video—Simplified

A simplified way to look at a music video is to consider the main attraction as one long scene of the band playing a song from beginning to end. Then you can use overwrite edits to cut away to shots other than the band that help tell your story. The video can cut back and forth between these two video tracks while the master music track remains intact. I said "simplified" because in reality, you will use lots of shots of the band, and you will use a variety of edits to achieve your goal. But when you look at a music video with this simplified view, it is easier to comprehend the task at hand.

Using Transitions and Effects

In addition to the basic cut from one scene to the next, a variety of transitions can be used instead. The most common one is the dissolve—one scene fading into another scene. In Figure 9.9, the image of the street is dissolving (sometimes called cross-dissolving) to an image of a sign that says "Los Gatos." There are other types of fades—fades from black, fades to black, or fades from and to white. But that's just the beginning. There are literally hundreds upon hundreds of transitions—wipes, splits, pushes, spirals—some of them must be seen to be understood.

Figure 9.9
One of the most common transitions is the dissolve, whereby one image fades into the next.

Special effects also abound in plentiful numbers—compositing, lightning, distortion, lens flare, warps, particle generators, and a lot more. These effects were once achieved only by using the tools of expensive video systems. Digital, computer-based, desktop video has made transitions—and special effects—much more accessible to budding filmmakers.

One word of caution: Don't overdo it. There is a tendency to overdo transitions and special effects because they're so cool. But once the effects become the focus of attention, you begin to lose the effectiveness of your music video. In general, effects should not call attention to themselves—they should enhance the story and experience that you are conveying in your video.

Considering Your Software Options

There are numerous choices in the realm of software for film and video production. This was not the case several years ago when the editing process was grueling, requiring several professional video machines, synchronization machines, numerous monitors, switchers, effects boxes, and a whole lot more. It has almost become cliché to say, "You have more computing power on your desktop than they had on the space shuttle." But you do. You have much, much more computing power than was imaginable when the space shuttle was launched.

Every industry has benefited from increased computing power, and audio, film, and video production is no exception. Even major motion pictures are often edited on computer-based machines, running software from companies such as Avid, Inc. and Apple.

Choosing Your Weapons

I'll start off by instigating a war: Mac or PC? PC or Mac? My computer is *way* better than your computer. Or is it?

The war of which computing platform is superior to any other is not the subject of this book. As a matter of fact, it's not the subject of many books at all these days, as the topic has worn itself out for lack of any true substance or meaning. Either platform is a good choice and is supported by tons of software to make your production a reality. Your choice may be guided by personal preference, by what you already own, or by your budget.

However (you knew there would be a "however," didn't you?), for the sake of the discussion here, I will focus on the Mac platform and its software. It is known for its user-friendliness and is being adopted in large numbers by amateurs and professionals alike for making video productions. Still, the same principles apply to both platforms; therefore, no one loses out in this discussion.

Editing Software

Although it's often referred to as editing software, the products that are available for production cover a lot more. Beyond the task of editing, there is color correction, transitions, titling, special effects, and more. These elements are fairly standard in most editing packages and are the ones you will find in Apple's Final Cut software. Final Cut comes in two flavors: Final Cut Pro and Final Cut Express (Final Cut Express is shown in Figure 9.10).

Aside from a large difference in the price tag, the differences between the two programs are not numerous. Final Cut Pro can do more in terms of batch processing lots of clips and offers other advantages such as keyframing capabilities, compatibility with Adobe After Effects plug-ins, support of additional video formats, and so on. At the end of the day, these features need not prevent you from creating professional results on Final Cut Express.

Figure 9.10
Apple's Final Cut and Final Cut Express (shown here) are two popular programs used for post-production video editing. *(Photo courtesy of Apple, Inc.)*

There is even a less expensive option if you choose to use Apple's iMovie to edit your project. The price tag on iMovie is hard to beat—it comes free and pre-installed with the purchase of any Mac. It is typically used by amateurs, hobbyists, or semi-professionals for basic editing projects. Now, someone, somewhere is likely to tell you something along the lines of, "You can *never* make a professional product using iMovie." But you know better by now, especially because of the word "never." Choose your weapons.

Editing on the Mac

Although I won't get into a full-blown lesson on using the Mac with either Final Cut or iMovie, a couple of general things are worth mentioning.

The first has to do with iMovie. Apple's iMovie is offered as part of a package called iLife, with other products in this suite, including iPhoto, iWeb, and Garage Band. When it was first released, iMovie was the only product that offered a way to work and play in the digital lifestyle we take for granted today. There have been successive versions of iMovie (that is, iLife) since its first release, and as of today's writing, the most current version is iLife 09.

I believe that most people will agree, and expect, that successive versions of software tend to improve in some way—ease of use, feature set, and so on. I am amazed to report to you that this did not happen with iMovie. Beginning with iMovie 08, Apple's mission seemed to center on turning iMovie into such a simple product that even a baby could make a movie with it. Well, a baby cannot make a movie with it, and neither can most people who have had any experience with video production software. Apple tried to even the score with iMovie 09 (shown in Figure 9.11)—and indeed, a few of the requested older features came back. But I am sad to say that I would never recommend iMovie 09 for any serious work.

All is not lost, however, because versions that precede iMovie 08 can be used effectively for editing without incurring a migraine headache. The headache is mostly caused by the lack of several standard features, the prime one being the *timeline*. There is no timeline in iMovie 09.

Figure 9.11
This screenshot of iMovie 09 shows several windows, but none of them contains an actual timeline.

More About the Timeline

The timeline is the central area that is most often used for editing video. It is a visual layout of the sequence of your video clips. It also gives you a visual reference of your audio and indicates where transitions or other special effects occur. You create the timeline by making all of these choices, but you are also free to change things around, reorder them, add to them, and so on. A timeline usually allows for several video tracks, some of which may be title overlays or special effects; and several audio tracks, some of which may be narration, source audio, music, and so on. A *playhead* moves from left to right in the timeline, represented by a vertical line, which plays everything back and also indicates where you are, from a timing standpoint, in your production. A timeline is an essential part of editing software for video, film, and even for multimedia presentations. Figure 9.12 shows the timeline in iMovie HD. The timeline is the row at the bottom of the window—in case you had any doubts, I even included the word "timeline" in the timeline!

Figure 9.12
Earlier versions of iMovie (in this case, iMovie HD), may not have the feature set of Final Cut, but at least it has a timeline, a feature that is essential.

SMPTE is a standard in film and video editing. The use of a timeline in video editing is a standard way of assembling clips into a video, with SMPTE being the master of where you are in time—expressed in minutes, seconds, and frames. Whatever software package you decide to use, I encourage you to stick with one that has a timeline. As you graduate to more sophisticated editing packages, you'll see that the timeline is always there as your main editing tool. Getting used to it now will help you in your current project as well as the ones you do down the road.

Throwing in the Kitchen Sync

Video equipment can range in price from hundreds of dollars to hundreds of thousands of dollars. I mention this now because of the topic of synchronization. The ease with which you can keep everything in sync, even when you're doing B-roll, cutaways, and many of the music video-editing techniques discussed previously, is somewhat determined by the sophistication of your gear. As an example, if you do a three-camera shoot, shoot lots of B-roll, and plan to use a lot of different takes within one scene, your need to have one timecode reference will be great—greater than a simple one-camera shoot with a few cutaways here or there. Sophisticated video gear or software helps simplify this process so that you can sync different shots with relative ease.

If you are on a lower budget, you know that at a minimum, your camcorder has timecode built in. If the other clips in your project don't include a corresponding timecode, then locking up and keeping in sync are a bit more challenging—but certainly not impossible.

This is one reason that I recommend that you include a reference track in your timeline that consists of a rough cut of the song (refer to Chapter 8, "The Video Process: Pre-Production and the Shoot," for more on a reference track). Beyond the master audio track, the reference track might provide clues as to who is singing what, where, and when. It might provide inspiration or ideas as you assemble your edits together, such as when you might cut away to a different shot or when you should stay put on the current shot. If you happen to have a reference track that has the exact timing of the master audio track, you are in better luck, because even without timecode on your B-roll footage, you can use the reference track to sync up *visually*—sort of an electronic lip-syncing as you cut to and from various shots. If the singer's lips are not in sync at any particular point, you can slide and adjust your audio or video tracks (or both) to make the sync work. The better video-editing software packages allow you to zoom in close to your audio waveform for making precise edits, as in Figures 9.13 and 9.14.

Figure 9.13
Final Cut allows you to take a close-up look at your audio waveform.

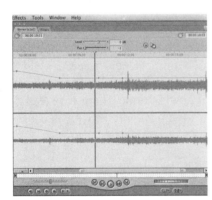

Figure 9.14
An even closer view of the audio waveform for making precise edits.

The other joy made possible by video-editing software is the ability to go back and make further changes at a later point in time. When you launch your video project on your computer, everything is in the same state that you left it last time. This allows you to further fine-tune your project or to create different versions if you so desire. Whatever the case, make sure you back up your project onto other drives or media, such as a DVD. Computers provide you with an amazing method of creating your music video. But computers also have an "amazing" way of losing important data when you need it. Back up. Enough said.

Wrapping Up

Although your editing chores may be over, your work is not. There are still a few points to keep in mind before you get your video on the Internet.

Color Correction

If you think back to the final mix of your song, you likely took great care to ensure that everything in the mix was just right. You probably took many passes and tweaked a lot of things on your tracks before you even came close to what you considered a final mix.

The same care must be taken with the video portion of your music video. Color correction, a subject beyond the scope of this particular book, is an important process—almost the equivalent of equalizing your mix. If you don't know enough about it or lack experience, you might consider hiring someone for that specific task. Though the ultimate differences may be subtle, a color-corrected video will have a much more professional look.

Titles

Most of your titles will be reserved for the end of your video. There is a fairly well-known practice of having a title section in the lower-left corner of a music video. These titles will include such information as the song title, performer, songwriter, record label (if there is one), and so on. Check out some music videos and look at how it's done. There are even some editing software programs that include a music video template into which you can plug your own copy.

The end titles or end credits of major motion pictures usually include members of the cast and crew. You might not find the same with music videos, although there are exceptions. You should make a final determination as to what to have for end credits as well as keeping in mind that it's not difficult to have a few versions—some with and some without end credits.

As with anything else, titles won't make or break your music video, but they will add a professional look (and give credit where credit is due).

Copyrights

Don't forget the legalese, especially when it comes to copyrights. If you are the copyright owner of the song, it should be stated at the end of your music video. If it is someone else's, you must acknowledged this person. This is for your own protection as well as the protection of those on your crew.

Looking at it from another angle, if you used any clips that are copyrights of other people, you must have permission to use them. If you think it's not that important because you're a little fish in the big sea, think again. Remember, your ultimate goal is to post your video on the Internet. If you do so without copyright permission, you're taking a big chance with your project and possibly with your career.

Final Review

When you're working on a project, do you hear a voice in your head? I'm not talking about multiple voices—if that's the case, you may have a lot of problems that we can't get into here. What I'm talking about is the voice that tells you "that doesn't sound right" or "that doesn't look right" and so on. It's your intuition on the deepest level. This voice is not the same voice that you use to try to convince yourself of something. This is a voice of reason, of objectivity—a voice that is dialed into all of your senses.

The thing is, you have a choice as to whether or not to listen to this voice.

My advice to you is that you should listen very carefully. And watch very carefully, too. Because many times, the difference between goodness and greatness lies in following through on what "the voice" is asking you to do. The enemy of the voice is laziness: "I know I should fix those two frames, but who's going to notice?" "Yeah, there's some kind of glitch at 01:03:21:07, but I can live with it." "I don't have time to reshoot that scene, so I'm going with what I've got."

It's those compromises that can sometimes get you into trouble, or at least, get you into a final product that is sub-par. It is often painful to have to do what your inner voice says is important, but if you're not stretching, if you're not pushing your own limits, then you are likely settling for something less.

The other part of this process is objectivity. It's very easy to get caught up in how good it sounds or how terrific it looks or how big of a yacht you're going to buy once this rakes in the dough. Become the listener. Take off your producer/songwriter hat and listen as if it's the first time you've ever heard or seen the music video. Maybe it really is great, but it will be up to others to pass final judgment on that—because if you're going to post a music video on the World Wide Web—others will be passing judgment on it.

Give your project 110 percent—or more. And when the time comes to review all of it, listen to your inner voice and also become a member of the audience. When you feel comfortable with your final music video, you're ready for the next step...posting it on the Internet, which I cover in Chapter 10, "Making Your Video Internet-Ready."

Part III

Posting Your Masterpiece on the Internet

Making Your Video
Internet-Ready

I COULD HAVE CALLED THIS chapter "Squeezing, Mangling, and Otherwise Reducing Everything You've Done to a Ridiculously Teeny, Tiny Size." But I didn't, and now, looking back, I'm glad I didn't, because it would have sounded odd—even though it is totally true.

The topics of compression and file formats come up again as you prepare your files for the Internet. I will also discuss uploading, downloading, streaming, tags, and keywords—all of which you'll need to understand when putting your music video on the Internet, or at the very least, you'll be able to use the terminology to impress your friends with a lot of techno-babble.

Revisiting Compression

Chapter 2, "Mixing Considerations," discussed the basics of compression, file formats, and so on. The last section of that chapter, "Compression Methods: The Bottom Line," discusses compression considerations after doing your final mix. Now I will delve into more detail, because when loading your video on the web, you need to take many different factors into account.

As a reminder, compression is used because of the large size of audio and video files. When you convert a WAV file to an MP3 file, you are using a special compression scheme that reduces the size of the file to one-tenth of its original size. Posting a music video on the web means creating video files that are small enough—but with good enough quality—that viewers can watch your video without it sputtering or freezing or crashing.

Video compression software examines each pixel of every frame and combines similar pixels together as a group. So, for example, if you have a close-up or medium shot of a lead singer with a static background (see Figure 10.1)—and assuming no other movement is in the shot except for the singer—the background will be analyzed and won't need to change from frame to frame. Only the singer's movements—facial and otherwise—need constant pixel updating. The static background essentially helps compress the video to a smaller size. However, I don't advise you to shoot your original video with that fact in mind. Shoot the best video you can, and if it requires a lot of movement, so be it.

Figure 10.1
A static background of an image does not need to change from frame to frame, which simplifies the compression process.

As I said in Chapter 2, QuickTime is a widely used format that is compatible with both Macs and PCs. But just to be clear (if that's even possible with this topic), there are such things as video compression formats, and there are also multimedia container formats—which can contain several different types of data (such as audio and video) using a compression scheme (codec) of some kind. Figure 10.2 illustrates QuickTime, the container format, "containing" an MPEG-4 video file and an AAC audio file.

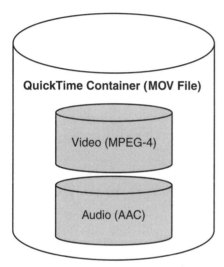

Figure 10.2
QuickTime container holds an MPEG-4 video file and an AAC audio file.

Different websites might have different requirements for the type of file you can upload. They may list as acceptable an MPEG-4 file and also a MOV file, which is a media container for QuickTime files. So what they're actually saying is that they accept files that are compressed with certain codecs as well as the final file formats.

On the support section of its website, Apple has an excellent article entitled "QuickTime 7: Preparing Your Movies for Internet Delivery." If you read this article and others like those listed in the upcoming section "Uploading to YouTube," you will have an excellent idea of what you need to do to prepare your video for the Internet. Figure 10.3 shows one of the capabilities of QuickTime—while it saves your video and audio settings, you can also specify Fast Start for Internet streaming.

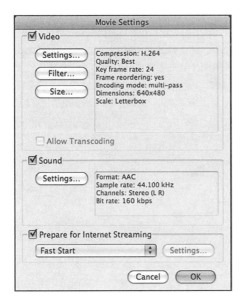

Figure 10.3
QuickTime lets you specify Fast Start for Internet streaming.

Uploading Your Video

You will need a high-speed Internet connection with good bandwidth to upload your video from your home computer to an Internet server. If you have only a dial-up connection, you'll have time to make an entirely new video by the time your music video uploads. Okay, so I exaggerate—but you get the idea. Hopefully, you have a cable modem, satellite, or DSL connection.

Aside from compression format (which includes a choice of video codecs and audio codecs), other considerations include screen size, aspect ratio, and bit rate.

A high bit rate is capable of containing more information, which translates into video quality. If you post your videos to YouTube and similar sites, they are going to reduce the bit rate according to their own standards. As such, I recommend using a high bit rate so that some semblance of quality video resolution remains after the various compression algorithms are applied.

Uploading to YouTube

Because YouTube is so ubiquitous and represents fairly standard specifications for video uploading, I have listed their requirements as an example of what you can expect:

> ▷ **Resolution and aspect ratio:** For Standard Definition (SD)—640 x 480 at 4:3 aspect ratio; for High Definition (HD)—1280 x 720 at 16:9 aspect ratio.

> ▷ **Bit rate:** No recommended value (get the best bit rate you can).

> ▷ **Frame rate:** The frame rate of the original video should be maintained.

> ▷ **Video codec:** H.264, MPEG-2, or MPEG-4.

> ▷ **Audio codec:** MP3 or AAC (Apple's codec).

> ▷ **Sampling rate:** 44.1 kHz.

> ▷ **Channels:** Two (stereo, left and right).

Other Flavors—Such as FLV

YouTube suggests on its website to use as little re-encoding as possible. In fact, YouTube will re-encode whatever you send them into FLV format. FLV was originally developed by Macromedia and later bought by Adobe. It is a container format that is optimized for playing via a Flash video player on the web. YouTube, Google Video, Yahoo!, and many others use this format. Because it is a plug-in, it's very easy to display video within a web page—and it offers a fast start-up time. And because it is a container format, it is compatible with several different codecs.

So, don't make your video as tiny as possible—it won't help anything and will actually do some harm to your resolution. Stick with YouTube's advice and encode once or twice if necessary.

Sorenson Compression

I want to mention one more thing regarding compression. If you use QuickTime as your file format, you will have choices of which codec to use—including H.264 and MPEG-4. You might also try the Sorensen video codec that Apple offers—it has a reputation for delivering very high quality. You can learn more about Sorensen video on its website, www.sorensonmedia.com.

Downloading and Streaming Your Video

When someone comes across a video on the web, it is usually streamed—meaning that it is played right then and there in real time. Although many videos *can* be downloaded, you must ask yourself if you *want* it to be downloaded. The rate at which web users can stream a video depends on the speed of their Internet connection. One user might be able to stream at 128 Kbps while other connections might be faster. The bottom line is that you want a fast start-up time. There was a day, a long time ago, when people were patient enough to wait a while for a video to start or a web page to load. No more. So, even if you decide to let web visitors download your video, make sure you allow for streaming as well. The cool trick about streaming is that the video file begins to play even before the entire file has been transmitted.

Tags, Keywords, and Searching

A tag is a descriptive keyword or group of keywords added to some form of content—and in this case, that would be video content. (In practice, the terms tags and keywords are sometimes used interchangeably). Tags work two ways—they convey more information about your video, and through search engines, provide more ways in which people can find you.

Imagine, for example, that your band, The Two Timers, creates a music video called *Father Time*, a heavy metal song about stopping the hands of time, your video might include images such as those in Figure 10.4. To tag this video, you need to start thinking about your images in a textual way—in other words, determine which keywords (or tags) would succinctly describe the images in your video, as well as your music and your band.

Here are some keywords you might consider for your band The Two Timers, as well as the song, *Father Time:*

Two Timers	Heavy Metal
Two	Heavy
Timers	Metal
Father Time	Music
Father	Band
Time	Clock
Hands of Time	Stop
Hands	

Figure 10.4
Try to think of all the keywords that have to do with your music video.

Notice how the keywords include a phrase, such as "Hands of Time," but also include the individual words. Most search engines can find phrases and the individual words that make them up. You also need to think of *context*—the words *music* and *band* are not necessarily in the lyrics of the song, but your video has a lot to do with those words, and they put everything in some sort of context.

If a potential fan heard about your song but only knew vaguely that it was heavy metal and had something to do with time, your music video would likely show up in a search.

Consider tags and keywords before you post your video online. Then when the time comes to actually post it, you are ready to be "found" by your fans.

Google has keyword tools that enable you to generate keyword ideas for your site and also to see what other, competitive sites are using for keywords. Best of all, there is no charge for this. You can start by Googling "Google keywords" and go from there.

There are also a large number of SEO (Search Engine Optimization) sites that can help you determine which keywords are relevant to you. As a matter of fact, you could spend 40 hours a week just studying these topics (but then you wouldn't have time to make music and music videos, so there's really no point to that). The full story on tagging, keywords, and search engine optimization certainly goes beyond the scope of this book, so I recommend using the Internet to find a vast array of articles on these topics, as well as the books you will find (on the Internet and in book shops) to get familiar with the tools that will promote your website and your music video.

Evaluating Popular

Online Sites

N OW THAT YOU'VE WATCHED your video a thousand times and know the details of every individual frame, it's time to share your creation with the rest of the world.

The Internet is in constant change as companies continue to expand their Internet presence and, in some cases, merge or acquire other companies. I mention that here because—in a few cases—what may be true as of this writing could be somewhat different when you read this book. Not too long ago, if you were talking about Google and YouTube, you were talking about two different companies. But this is no longer true because Google acquired YouTube, although Google has kept YouTube's name and identity intact. Also, as of this writing, discussing Microsoft and Yahoo! is discussing two different companies, but by the time you read this book—who knows? Maybe a merger will have formed a new MicroHoo.

Why is this important to you? Because now you are about to put on your business hat and take on the job of marketing your music video. As such, you need to be aware of who's who and what's what. Some of that information is in this chapter, but because of the ever-changing nature of the Internet, you will be wise to consistently search and research the web to see what kinds of developments are taking place on the Internet and how they might affect your marketing efforts.

Why Not Post on Your Own Site?

If you have your own website, you *should* post your video there. What is important to realize is that there is a difference in posting to an online site and posting on your own site in terms of purpose, strategy, and expectations.

When you post to a popular online site, your purpose is building awareness. You are essentially casting a wide net to get as many eyeballs as possible viewing your site and video. This is not to say that you don't want a large number of visitors coming to your own site. But your site probably doesn't have as large an audience as YouTube does, for example. Your site has a different purpose, which is converting newcomers to fans and converting existing fans into more loyal fans.

A popular site is the right environment for sharing content with others and thus provides a "viral" venue for marketing. Your own site is better suited for delving deeper into your band's players, history, and additional music; and your site can provide you with a means to sell your own CDs, T-shirts, and coffee mugs. Your site can create a "call to action" that you cannot easily create from a YouTube video.

On the other hand, a popular online site has very limited customization options. Your own site can be customized any way you want in look, feel, and purpose. You have creative control of your own site, but not of a popular online site.

So, the obvious answer is that *you do both*—you use popular online sites as well as your own site to host your video and increase your audience.

Categories of Sites

Posting your music video on the Internet is not as straightforward as finding music video sites and uploading your video. As a matter of fact, there is no such category as music video sites. There are a few different types of sites that will be able to accommodate you, but they fall into different categories. Also, a ton of sites are dedicated to hosting video, but only those of a political or journalistic nature. Ourmedia.org, FreeVlog.org, and Spot.us are only a few examples of the multitude of sites that are very open to new media, but not to music media. So, because your focus is on music, take a look at sites that are open to hosting music videos.

Multipurpose Sites

A multipurpose site is any site that allows—as its general focus—the uploading of videos. This means all types of videos, whether it is a music video or a video of a cat playing a keyboard or flushing a toilet. Generally speaking, anything goes. The first site that comes to mind, naturally, is YouTube, the grandfather of all video websites.

YouTube

YouTube is the dominating force behind online video. By August 2009, the number of videos watched on Google sites reached more than ten billion, with YouTube responsible for virtually all of that number. During the same time period, YouTube accounted for 40 percent of all videos watched on the Internet. Although I can't say how many of those videos were music videos, I can say that YouTube's closest competitors reach only single-digit percentages of all videos watched on the web.

 Because YouTube is meant for the uploading and viewing of endless types of videos, it has video categories of its own—and *lots* of them. These include News & Politics, Sports, Entertainment, Film & Animation, and many more.

The good news is that there is a category or channel called *Music.* The bad news is that this category is subdivided into additional ones such as Top Music, Top Indie Music, Top Major Label Music, Rising Videos, Most Viewed, and so on. To look at this another way, just because you upload your music video to YouTube doesn't mean your music will end up being located right next to Madonna's latest hit. The only category that you can count on—as an unsigned artist—is Top Unsigned Music.

"YouTube is the new MTV."

–Al Yankovic

How can you increase your chances that your video will be seen on YouTube?

Increasing Your Views on YouTube

When you create your own website, there is no guarantee that anyone will visit it. You must find a way to create traffic to your site. The same holds true for YouTube; just because you post a video doesn't mean that people will know it exists.

The best thing you can do is *be very active* on YouTube. You want to create as many "views" as possible to increase your ranking on YouTube. To get more views, you must take advantage of a variety of YouTube features.

▷ **Post videos.** Post your music video, but think about additional videos such as interviews with band members and fans, a "making of" video, and so on. Visitors will be able to see that you have other videos beyond the music video they're watching.

▷ **Comment on other videos.** Try to stick to positive comments. When other people read comments, they will have the option to click on your username and go immediately to your music video page.

▷ **Be a friend.**

▷ **Subscribe to other users' pages.**

▷ **Get involved in discussions.** Get on a "most discussed" list.

▷ **Create tutorial videos of your own.** You might even create one on how to make a music video and post it online. Posting a tutorial video is part of an overall strategy to make yourself more visible on YouTube.

Embed This

One of the great things about the Internet is the ease with which you can share things (music, photos, videos, and so on) with other people via other websites. YouTube, like many other social websites, includes two boxes containing code—one named *URL* and the other named *Embed,* shown in Figure 11.1. The URL is, as you expect, the exact link to the page you're on—in your case, your music video page. The Embed code allows you to embed code on other websites (yours, for certain), resulting in the video appearing on those sites. So, if you want to have your music video on YouTube, your own website, your MySpace page, and so on, uploading only one time and re-using the embed code will allow you to embed your video on all of these sites, and some others as well.

You may discover that there are also many "underhanded ways" or tricks that you can do to increase your views. My advice is to keep away from those and stay legit. You'll be able to increase your views, your ranking, and your traffic, by using all the previously mentioned methods, and you won't risk being banned from certain search engine sites like Google.

Video-Specific Sites

Some sites are specifically designed to host videos. One site that immediately comes to mind is Veoh—not to be confused with Vimeo, although they aren't that different from one another.

Figure 11.1
Posting video on YouTube provides you with embed code and a direct URL to your page.

Veoh allows you to upload videos to your own Veoh account. It includes embed codes, links, and so on, just like YouTube. This site, like most of the others, lets you organize your video into groups or categories—and one of the groups is Music. Doing this will likely make your video easier to find. Also, if you have a video over a gigabyte in size, Veoh provides a special uploading tool that uploads a large file in 256KB chunks. The significance here is that most of the video-hosting sites don't accommodate files this large (unless, of course, you upgrade to the premium package, which allows you to do most everything you'd like, including hosting large video files).

 Vimeo also includes the expected set of features—embedding, sharing, and along with the trend in social websites, a method to vote for or "like" a particular video. Groups and channels are also available.

A trend that I'm seeing in these two sites and many others is the tendency to be somewhat like Hulu.com. Hulu.com is a video-hosting site, too, but for the big players—catering to the major television networks and cable outlets, as well as many motion picture studios.

Hulu hosts everything from short clips to full television episodes to full-length motion pictures. The thing is, Hulu is not going to host video for *us*—the "little guys." That's not its intent or purpose. It is essentially an Internet outlet for major television and motion picture productions.

Although Veoh and Vimeo do host us little guys, I'm sensing that they (and other video sites) are trying to be a "Hulu for Music" site. You can see the stature of the artists that Veoh is promoting on their main page for Music, shown in Figure 11.2. I hope that these sites don't become so major league that they stop hosting up-and-coming artists. There are not a lot of options for independent artists, and contrary to what many people might think, the majority of sites for indies are music sites *only*—they aren't hosts for music *videos*.

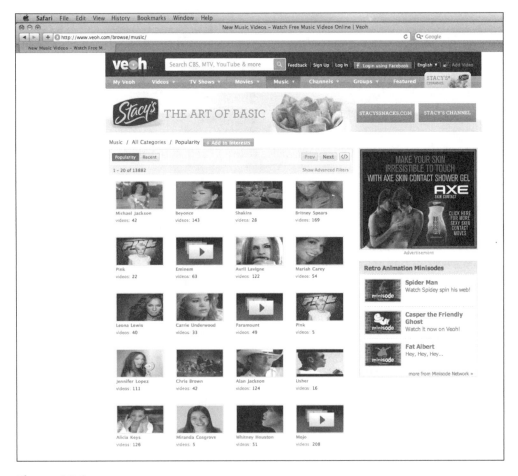

Figure 11.2
Veoh's music page shows its impressive list of artists.

One site that is known for catering to indie music videos is Pitchfork.tv. It is a site that reviews independent music and also hosts videos. It is viewed by some as a blessing and by others as a curse, in that Pitchfork.tv can either make or break new artists. If you have an indie band slant, you might want to investigate it.

Other sites are available for uploading your video, but their slants are different. Some of them may favor journalistic or how-to videos, whereas others, such as Blip.tv, are outlets for "webisodes."

Another interesting site you may want to check out is Dailymotion.com. Its tag line is "What good is a video, if it's stuck on your camera, hard drive, or mobile phone?" It seems to be targeting everyone and anyone who wants to upload video in a variety of categories, some of which are shown in Figure 11.3.

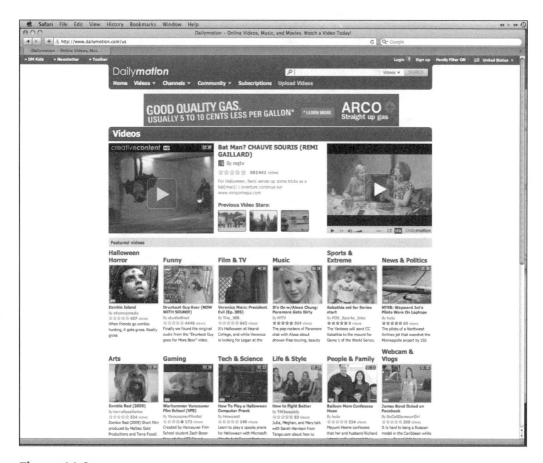

Figure 11.3
Dailymotion has tons of categories or channels and may be a good place to upload your music video.

In terms of just hosting a video that you know you'll embed somewhere else, a site like Photobucket may be a good choice. Which site is right for you depends greatly on whether you simply want a place to park your video (such as Photobucket) or a place that is more of a *destination*—where visitors will come to see your video.

Social Networking Sites

Social networking sites have experienced rapid growth over the past couple of years. Originally intended simply as a way to stay connected to friends and family, these sites have become platforms for promoting one's music, videos, music videos, careers, and a lot more.

MySpace and Facebook

As you will see, dozens of social networking sites can give you a means for posting your music video, but they are not music video sites per se. (It would be nice to discover a site that was actually set up for this purpose.) Yes, there are *music* sites that are designed to host your music while including the social networking features as well, but there are no *music video* sites that are streamlined enough to make the process easy.

Two of the most popular social networking sites, MySpace and Facebook (shown in Figures 11.4 and 11.5), can accommodate your music as well as your music videos. Although both are general-purpose social-networking sites, MySpace has lately focused more of its energies on being a music-oriented site. At the same time, many observers have noted that MySpace has fallen in overall popularity recently while Facebook has done quite the opposite.

If you were to post a video on MySpace as most people do (using the Video menu of your profile), your video would be posted, it just wouldn't appear on your main page. Some people choose to post videos on their blog. It's common to upload a video to YouTube and then copy the embedded video into one's blog. But, again, the video will appear on your blog and not on your main MySpace page.

Figure 11.4
MySpace homepage.

Figure 11.5
Facebook homepage.

The way to make your music video appear on your main MySpace page is to embed the Embed code (sounds redundant, I know, but you know what I mean) into the section of your profile known as Musician Details. (Refer to Figure 11.1 to see the Embed code.) Oh, did I forget to mention that you must have an Artist Profile to do this? If you don't have that, you will not have some of the features you will need, so it's best to set your profile this way (yes, even if you have to start over).

Facebook also has a video-uploading feature along with tags that others can search through. When you use Facebook, your video will appear on your profile as a small-sized still image until it's clicked—then it turns into a larger motion video that plays right on the same page, as seen in Figure 11.6.

Figure 11.6
Click on a Facebook video, and
it enlarges and plays in place.

Both Facebook and MySpace use their own compression algorithms to squeeze your video into a smaller file. You'll notice this right away because you will see the loss in quality on your video. The good news is that they are programmed to play almost immediately; in other words, visitors don't have to sit and wait for a large file to download to their computers.

Neither site wants adult content on their pages, and many sites are also vigilant about making sure you own the copyright to the material. Some sites are stricter than others about policing their sites, but almost all of them ask you to agree to a statement, upon uploading your video, that you are the copyright owner and that you are not uploading adult content to the site.

Get Embed with This, Widget

Not very long ago, most websites lived in their own little room with their own little toys. Then one day Facebook enabled you to link content to MySpace, and then MySpace enabled you to link your video to Facebook. On and on it went, until now we can all link our sites to one another. Often these sites have *widgets,* which are little pieces of code that enable you to create these links between sites easily (providing you have the right username and password for the site to which you are linking).

What this means is that you can save a lot of time and trouble by taking advantage of these widgets. And the more you link content from one site to another to another to another, the more likely you will raise your own ranking in search engines, including Google (which links to…oh well, don't get me started).

The linking together of various sites has proliferated so much that sites like CNN.com link to Facebook. It is no longer a novelty to embed your widget all over the place. Just choose your places carefully, and make sure they represent the style and image you want to project.

Social Networking/Video Hybrids

I call iMeem, shown in Figure 11.7, and many other sites like it, *hybrid* sites. Do they stream videos? Yes. Are there social networking features built in? Yes. Would these sites be ideal for posting your music video? No.

This site and similar ones definitely leverage the advantages of social media such as making friends, rating videos, recommending videos, and so on. But as I mentioned earlier in this chapter when discussing Hulu.com, these sites are not really geared for turning unknown artists into superstars. They will allow superstars to become *bigger* superstars. Perhaps they didn't start that way, but many hybrids are becoming destinations for more professional artists rather than for unknown or indie artists.

Some sites may or may not have an emphasis on social networking but also boast video reviews and rankings. One such site is Metacafe.com, which emphasizes the short-form video, with the average length being 90 seconds. That's short even by music video standards.

Figure 11.7
iMeem is a nice hybrid site, but isn't ideal for posting music videos.

Metacafe has strict User Submission Guidelines, some of which cause me to recommend avoiding this site altogether. The guidelines have to do with intellectual rights and copyrights. For example—and I apologize for the length of this quote (but it's actually only one sentence)—here is an excerpt from its user submissions section:

> *You retain all of your ownership rights in your User Submissions. However, by submitting the User Submissions to Metacafe, you hereby grant Metacafe, in addition to any other rights which it has pursuant to any other program established by Metacafe, a worldwide, non-exclusive and transferable license to use, copy, prepare derivative works of (including without limitation, to rename, edit, shorten, split the videos into different segments, and use the entire video or segments as part of compilations), display, and perform the User Submissions in connection with the Website and Metacafe's (and its successor's) business, including without limitation to grant access to the Website to third parties to view the User Submission (and derivative works thereof).*

I won't get into an in-depth discussion about law here, but suffice it to say that you don't really want to do any of these things. If you are serious about your music video production, you don't want to authorize derivative works, including the right for them to edit your video to tiny pieces. You also don't want to grant rights like these to successor's businesses or other third parties. Oh, and you don't want to grant a worldwide *transferable* license.

But don't feel disappointed. After scouring through the Metacafe site, I was unable to find any real music videos. You should evaluate it for yourself, as with any site, to see if it fits your needs.

A Different Type of Music Video Site

During the course of writing this book, I came across a site called Radar Music Videos (see Figure 11.8). This UK–based company is in the business of putting together music video directors with bands or other artists. Its reason for existence is based upon how difficult it is for artists to produce professional music videos, let alone know where to post them to get maximum exposure. To simplify how this works, you post a "brief" or short summary describing what your music video is about, upload relevant information, and then scout and select a music video director based upon the treatments you receive.

Figure 11.8
Radar Music Videos is a site with a total focus on making music videos and posting them online.

You are able to see directors' blogs, show reels, and previous music videos. The directors also have a rating based upon previous video success, view counts, awards, and so on. You select a director to work with, and when your music video is completed, you can promote it by building playlists, friend lists, and exposing it to Radar's entire network of members. Radar editors also view the videos, some of which are selected for its Featured section. Wider exposure is achieved through relationships with other sites (many of which I've already mentioned) so that you have the widest distribution possible.

If you are interested in this approach, I encourage you to visit www.radarmusicvideos.com to better understand its business model and to see if it's a good fit for you. I have not had personal experience with Radar as I have just discovered it, but I was impressed that someone recognized the need for having a true focus on the making and distribution of music videos online.

What Kind of Site Is This, Anyway?

When you delve into the world of websites that may become distribution points for your music video, you will discover an almost endless universe of little sites, big sites, unknown sites, up-and-coming sites, famous sites, and infamous sites. There are many more beyond the ones mentioned in this chapter, and even more new sites will exist by the time you read this book. That's why one of your tasks is to always investigate, in detail, what kind of site you are considering for posting your video. Investigate everything, from the image you want to project to the type of online agreement you're willing to sign. Do your homework first, before registering with a new or unknown website.

Working with
iTunes Videos

HERE'S A QUESTION I ASKED MYSELF when organizing my thoughts for writing this book: Is the proliferation of iTunes, iPods, and iPhones so ubiquitous that it deserves its own section in this book?

Naturally, you can see that the answer was "yes."

This is not to say that the processes involved for converting, downloading, synching, and otherwise managing video for iTunes and its supported devices is difficult. It just has its own set of requirements that you ought to know and understand.

So, where should you start? Start by asking yourself some important questions:

▷ Are you going to want videos to play not only on iTunes, but also on iPods, iPhones, and Apple TV?

▷ Do you know which file format your video must be converted to in order to play nicely with iTunes and its supported devices?

▷ Are you starting with an already completed QuickTime video (which works on both Mac and PC platforms), or do you want to export your final file from iMovie or Final Cut Pro (or Final Cut Express) on the Mac platform?

▷ Are you a PC user who will need to convert to the iTunes format using PC software (if you're not using QuickTime Pro for conversation)?

As you've likely surmised, these are issues you'll want to be clear on before you go about converting, compressing, or otherwise manipulating video files.

Determining the Target

One might suppose the easiest thing in the world would be to drop any video file onto iTunes and Bam!—it's ready to view. In reality, iTunes plays only a few file formats—and iPods and iPhones play even fewer. (You can drop a QuickTime file directly into iTunes, and it will play without any additional effort on your part.)

As you know from previous chapters that discussed file formats, your original video might be in DV or MPEG-2 format (camcorder), and if you're talking about converting from a DVD, it also is in MPEG-2 format. On the other hand, videos on the Internet can be in WMV, DivX, or QuickTime format, to name a few. And, odd as it may seem, you cannot play a QuickTime video on iPods or other portable devices without some conversion taking place.

So, starting with the lowest common denominator, there are two file types that play on portable devices such as iPods and iPhones:

▷ MPEG-4

▷ H.264

That's it—that's the end of the list. So if you're sure—or even mildly convinced—that you will want a video that ultimately can be played on an iPod or iPhone, converting to this format is in your future, or at least *part* of your future. Having said that, there are lots of ways of preparing a suitable file, and they boil down to two choices—using Apple's QuickTime Pro or using a third-party software solution.

Which File Format Is Best—MPEG-4 or H.264?

When you are converting video files to play on devices with tiny screens, you might assume that it is not critical whether you choose MPEG-4 or H.264 as your file format. Although the quality differences may be difficult (for some) to ascertain, most professionals do agree that the H.264 file format not only gives a boost in quality but also produces a smaller file size. All of the videos on Apple's iTunes store use the H.264 format. When you consider that, plus the possibility that your video files may be used elsewhere (beyond the iPod), the H.264 file format seems to be the clear winner.

Converting Your Files

If you were thinking "enough with all of these conversions and file formats," then you have a couple of choices. One, you might take this idea and start a standup comedy routine, or two—and the much easier choice—use QuickTime Pro for your conversions. The good news is that QuickTime Pro is very intuitive and extremely easy to use.

Converting with QuickTime Pro

The easiest way to get from here to there, assuming you already have a finished QuickTime file (MOV) in your possession, is to use Apple's QuickTime Pro. QuickTime Pro is a piece of software you always want to have on hand and always updated as new versions are released. For QuickTime Pro to work properly, you must have version 7.03 or later.

Always use the *absolute latest version* of QuickTime Pro.

Converting your file to a format for the iPod is very simple. After opening your file, you choose Export from the File menu, as shown in Figure 12.1.

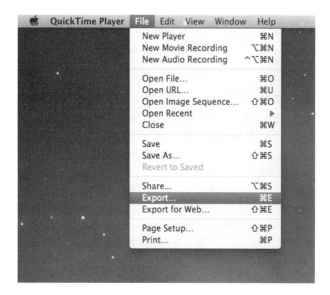

Figure 12.1
To convert a file for the iPod,
use QuickTime's Export option.

Then, from the Export option, choose Movie to iPod from the drop-down menu, as shown in Figure 12.2.

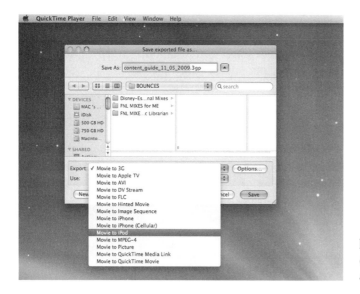

Figure 12.2
QuickTime provides
a Movie to iPod option.

Once the conversion is done, click on Save, and a new file is placed on your desktop by default, or any other location that you choose. This file is now playable on your iPod.

Follow the remaining steps to place the movie on your iPod:

1. Click on the file and watch to make sure the conversion was successful.

2. Open iTunes.

3. Drag the new file into your iTunes Library or the playlist of your choice.

4. Hook up the iPod to your computer and sync up as you usually do to get the movie onto your iPod.

Converting Directly from iMovie

If your music video is in iMovie, you can make it iTunes- and iPod-ready directly from the application. For this to work seamlessly, Apple states that you must have QuickTime 7.03 or later and iTunes 6 or later.

If you're exporting from iMovie HD 6, you use the Share menu and then select iPod. The application compresses the file and automatically saves it to your iTunes Library. After that, you simply synch up with your iPod, and you are set to go.

In iMovie HD 5, the process is similar, with a couple of additional steps. After selecting the Share menu, you click on the QuickTime tab, choose Expert Settings, and then select Movie to iPod 320 x 240 in the Export drop-down menu. The movie will be saved to the hard disk location of your choice. After that (and after viewing the movie in QuickTime to ensure it is to your liking), drag the file into your iTunes Library.

However, iMovie 09 adds some coolness to the mix. There is now a Share menu item in some of Apple's applications, including iMovie 09. If you're using this version (and presumably, later ones as well), you choose Export, which is accessible from the Share menu, as shown in Figure 12.3.

Figure 12.3

Many newer Mac applications include a Share menu, as shown here in iMovie 09.

When you select Export, you are presented with a very cool grid that shows you to which devices you can target, such as iPod, iPhone, Apple TV, YouTube, and so on (see Figure 12.4). In addition, you can select the size and aspect ratio of the exported movie. In essence, all the work is done for you, once you've determined what you want as your final output.

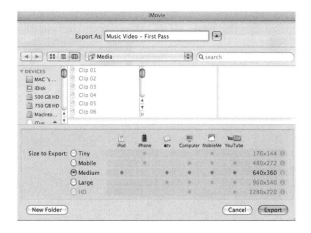

Figure 12.4
A wide number of options are readily available on a grid in iMovie's Export menu.

Converting Directly from Final Cut

Final Cut Pro 7 and Final Cut Express 4 (the latest versions as of this writing) from Apple include a customizable sharing option that provides exporting to formats suitable for YouTube, iPhone, iPod, and Apple TV. In addition to creating the correct formats for these targets, you can select post-compression "Job Actions" that *import directly* into iTunes, synch to iPod or iPhone, publish to YouTube, and so on, leaving you free to eat your dinner, buy new software online, or whatever suits you. However, these actions can take place in the background, leaving you free to work in Final Cut or any other application for that matter. (You may not have an excuse to buy that software after all.)

Earlier versions of Final Cut offered conversion to iPod format by selecting the Export option from the File menu and then the Using QuickTime Conversion option, as shown in Figure 12.5.

From the Using QuickTime Conversion option, you can select iPod and choose where to save the file, as shown in Figure 12.6.

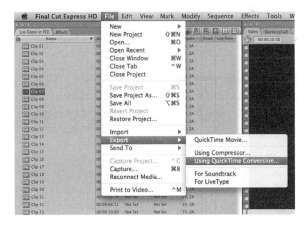

Figure 12.5

Earlier versions of Final Cut did not have a Share menu, but used the Export option to create different formats.

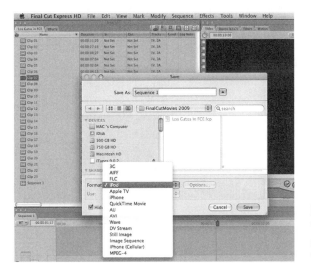

Figure 12.6

The Using QuickTime Conversion option allows you to select the iPod as your final destination.

As in previous cases, the remaining steps are the same:

1. Click on the file and watch to make sure the conversion was successful.

2. Open iTunes.

3. Drag the new file into your iTunes Library or the playlist of your choice.

4. Hook up the iPod to your computer and sync up as you usually do to get the movie onto your iPod.

Because of the numerous versions of software, including iMovie and Final Cut, coupled with the multiple types of iPods, from Classics to Third Generation to Fifth Generation to iPod Touch, and ditto for iPhones, your mileage may differ. What I mean is that the software requirements, the menu choices, and even the playability of video on earlier iPods will vary greatly. It's wise to know the versions of your software and hardware and then use the Internet to search for solutions that fit your specific situation.

Using Third-Party Options

There are other software exporting options beyond Apple's QuickTime Pro. Many companies have developed software for this purpose for both the Mac and the PC, and often for both platforms. Some of them are freeware, some are shareware, and none of them is expensive. Some professionals believe that these other options work faster than QuickTime Pro, but I can't attest to that.

Here are some examples of third-party software available for Mac and PC platforms. (This list is for reference and not as an endorsement by the author or publisher.)

▷ **Mac and Windows**

- Videora

- HandBrake

▷ **Windows Only**

- AVS Video Converter

- MadZ Video to iPod Converter

- Xilisoft iPod Video Converter

▷ **Mac Only**

- ViddyUp (formerly known as Podner)

- MoviesForMyPod

- Video2Pod

Managing Music Videos on iTunes

As a general rule, iTunes recognizes three main video categories: movies, TV shows, and music videos. Content that is purchased from the iTunes store is already tagged according to these categories and placed into their respective folders. However, when you drag or import videos of your own into iTunes, they are categorized as movies by default and are given a title based upon the original filename. Other data, the kind that automatically resides in movies and television shows purchased from the iTunes store, is missing and must be filled in by you. The process of describing the type of video is called *tagging.*

The process of tagging in most other situations on the Internet means supplying a host of keywords relevant to your content—whether that content is video, books, blogs, and so on. Within iTunes, tagging means classifying your media by selecting the right Media Kind, offering you the choices of movie, TV show, or music video. These choices were available in iTunes 7 under the Video tab, whereas with iTunes 8 and later, you choose the right Media Kind from the Options tab. (See Figures 12.7 and 12.8.) To get to this Options tab, you first right-click or control-click on your video in the movies section of iTunes and choose Get Info. From there, seven tabs are presented, including Options.

Figure 12.7
The Options menu is available in iTunes after choosing Get Info.

Figure 12.8
There are several ways to categorize Media Kind, including Music Video.

Music videos, oddly enough, are not listed separately in iTunes as music videos. When your selection for Media Kind is changed to music videos, your content will no longer appear in Movies. It will be in the Music section of iTunes, right by your music tracks that are audio only. So, it can be a bit awkward to categorize your video as a music video, click OK, and then watch as it disappears from your list of movies. The system is obviously not perfect, but it's also improving as time goes by. It may even be a different story by the time you read this.

In a nutshell, tagging in iTunes is a determining factor as to where your video content will appear in iTunes and/or your iPod. The exact menu choices and categorization methods vary slightly with different version of iTunes and iPods, so it's best to consult your manual (or conduct an Internet search) to find out which one fits your situation.

Transferring Videos to the iPod

After tagging your video, you will likely want to transfer it to your iPod so that you can take it with you. If iTunes is set up to use manual synchronization, you simply drag and drop the content to the iPod after it's connected. Automatic syncing for the different video categories is controlled by the relevant configuration tabs that are available in iTunes during the syncing process.

Just like other content in your iTunes Library, videos will respond to the Only Sync Checked Items option (under the Summary tab), so make sure that it's enabled.

As you can see, working with iTunes videos reveals a number of issues to take into account, from what your final target device (or software) will be to the different ways that software programs deal with converting your final music video.

Marketing Your

Music Video

THE EFFECTS OF THE INTERNET and digital media on our lives have been so profound that it's difficult to summarize it in a sentence, a paragraph, or a book. That's partly because we are in the eye of this storm of change. The Internet has changed the way we communicate, the way we create, the way we educate, and the way we entertain. One thing is certain—the Internet has forever changed the music business, from the creative process to the way we market new music to others. This book has thus far dealt with the former, and now it is time to address the latter.

This chapter includes a discussion of traditional marketing and social marketing. There are some who believe the newer social marketing, which includes leveraging sites such as MySpace, Facebook, Twitter, and a whole lot more, are not only the wave of the future, but also simultaneously relegate traditional marketing to the distant past. And there are others, including this author, who believe that a combination of traditional and social marketing is the best formula for success.

One thing I've learned over the years is that it's tempting to throw the proverbial baby out with the bathwater. I was working for Microsoft when CD-ROMs first debuted and everyone hailed the end of printed books. Obviously, that didn't happen, and the two media have coexisted for many years, each having its own distinct advantages.

Now, if someone were really brilliant back in the day, they would have known that CD-ROMs weren't the threat—the Internet and portable devices were the threat. Of course, that was a long time ago, and no one could see it coming. Likewise, we can't be certain what the marketing process will really look like 20 years from now. And so, because I believe in a combination of traditional and social marketing, I offer you information on both methods and how they can be used together.

If You Post It, Will They Come?

The answer, in a word, is no—not necessarily. (Yes, I know, that's three words.) The saying has many variations based on the original—"If you *make* it, will they come?" The "it" might refer to any type of product from software to computer hardware to a new type of toaster. The phrase is often heard in the halls of marketing departments where product managers and product developers are in heated debates about the chances of their product's success. The old school of thought states that if a product is good enough, people obviously will buy it. The newer school states that unless some significant marketing energy is put behind a product (or service, for that matter), the chances of success are very limited, no matter how good the product actually is.

I suggest that marketing effort is not a luxury but a necessity in the music business, and that certainly applies to getting your music video seen and heard.

I Have Some Good News and Some Bad News

The good news is that the Internet has changed all the rules. Now, instead of a few select artists being lucky enough to have a record contract, the playing field is wide open. With the Internet, it is now possible for one act to be marketed to millions of people, record label not required. Sure, small independent labels may be effective in this new arena, but the days of major corporations being a necessary part of the record-making machine seem to be pretty much over.

The bad news is everything I just wrote in the preceding paragraph. Because the playing field is wide open, the Internet is flooded with acts of all kinds and all levels of experience vying for the attention of those millions of prospective listeners. Maybe it's true that major labels are a thing of the past, but those same labels acted as a filter of sorts so that *some* level of quality and professionalism was present in the artists who made it to the surface. The often-used distribution models of one-to-many or many-to-one can be applied to the way music industry distribution has changed over the years, as shown in Figure 13.1. The old record industry allowed a few artists to reach many people. The current digital music industry has an overabundance of artists, but they're able to reach only smaller portions of the audience. The ideal of the future would be many artists having the ability to reach many people.

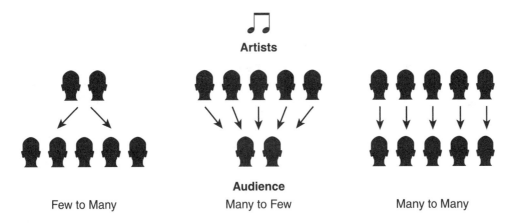

Figure 13.1
From left to right, the first diagram represents the "old" model of music distribution, the second is the current digital music distribution, and on the right is the hopeful future.

All of this is to say that marketing now plays a more significant role—not that it didn't have an important role before—but perhaps now, more than ever, a *strategic* marketing mix has become a necessity, especially in light of new marketing methods.

Understanding the Marketing Mix

The marketing mix has traditionally consisted of "The Four Ps"—Product (or service), Place, Price, and Promotion. Simply put, it means putting out the right product at the right time and place and at the right price point. These Four Ps correspond to the formal definition of the marketing mix (see Figure 13.2).

FOUR Ps

Product	Place	Price	Promotion

Figure 13.2
A classic definition of the marketing mix describes marketing strategy in terms of "The Four Ps."

There are other definitions of the marketing mix as well. From a tactical point of few, it can be considered as a combination of different marketing methods and techniques. It can be your marketing communications strategy, directing your message to your prospective customer (or fan) from all sides. Some have called this approach 360 degree marketing, although you can find dozens of other versions of what 360 degree marketing is supposed to mean. Figure 13.3 represents just one of them.

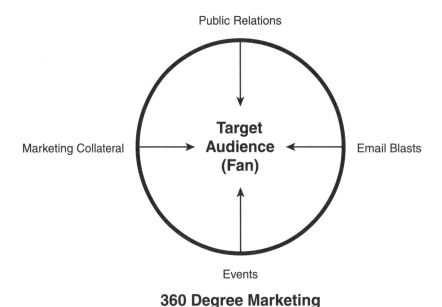

360 Degree Marketing
or Integrated Marketing Communications

Figure 13.3
This is one of the models of the term "360 degree marketing," combining different marketing techniques to reach your target audience.

For the purposes of this book, I'm going to look at the marketing mix through a contemporary lens. I will view traditional marketing as all of the "old school" marketing methods, from positioning to PR to promotion. Social marketing will include such phenomena as MySpace, Facebook, Twitter, blogs, forums, and the like.

Somewhere between traditional and social marketing there was the practice of viral marketing or guerilla marketing, mostly utilizing websites and email as marketing tools. This was *before* social marketing and serves as a good example of a transition period between the old and the new marketing methods. These concepts are illustrated in Figure 13.4.

Figure 13.4
An illustration of traditional marketing, social marketing, and the transition that occurred between the two.

Now, take a look at traditional marketing and social marketing and see if it doesn't make sense to create a formula for an even newer marketing mix. This mix might consist of a combination of traditional marketing, viral marketing, email marketing, social network marketing, and more—but likely will involve some of each.

A discussion of the fine details of every marketing tactic you can use, whether traditional, social, or a mix of both, is beyond the scope of this book. At a higher level is the need to have an understanding of marketing concepts. Once you understand those, you can determine which ones apply to you and then use your creativity to create a marketing plan of your own.

Traditional Marketing

Traditional marketing is the marketing we and our parents and their parents grew up with. According to the American Marketing Association, it is "the process for creating, communicating, delivering, and exchanging offerings that have value for customers, clients, partners, and society at large." If that sounds a bit corporate, that's because it is. Several of the processes that comprise traditional marketing might apply to large businesses and corporations, whereas others have validity for us, the makers of music videos.

Traditional marketing in a company usually includes activities such as developing a mission statement, positioning, market segmentation, value proposition, branding, public relations or publicity, promotion, and advertising. Sounds like this is the corporate stuff, right? Well, not necessarily—not when you understand how these things may apply an individual level.

The Mission Statement

A mission statement accurately describes why a company or organization exists and what it hopes to accomplish in the future. It's a description of its purpose—its reason for being.

Mission statements can sometimes be a mouthful because marketers want to make sure that everything about the company is summarized in one paragraph. Sometimes the statement is full of jargon, but here's an example of a simple one from The Coca-Cola Company:

The Coca-Cola Promise: The Coca-Cola Company exists to benefit and refresh everyone it touches. The basic proposition of our business is simple, solid, and timeless. When we bring refreshment, value, joy, and fun to our stakeholders, then we successfully nurture and protect our brands, particularly Coca-Cola. That is the key to fulfilling our ultimate obligation to provide consistently attractive returns to the owners of our business.

Sometimes a company's mission statement is summarized in one line. For example, the mission statement of Starbuck's Coffee is "To inspire and nurture the human spirit—one person, one cup, and one neighborhood at a time."

Now, how does a mission statement apply to you? On an individual level, your mission statement might be as follows: "My mission is to grow personally, professionally, and emotionally by using my unique perspective and my belief in others' inherent goodness and integrity." Sounds simple, but to do this daily and on a consistent basis might be difficult. That's what mission statements are for—they remind us why we do what we do so that we stay focused on our main objective.

An artist can have a mission statement. A band can have a mission statement—perhaps something like this:

Our mission is to provide life-long entertainment experiences for our community, country, and planet, through the performance of original music, music videos, and live concerts. In the course of achieving our goals, we will be an example of good teamwork and friendship, resolving any internal disputes or obstacles that might get in our way. While competing at the highest level in the entertainment industry, we will provide opportunities for others to share our experience whether they are a fan or a part of our extended team.

A business or enterprise usually publishes its mission statement in its marketing literature and on its website. You, as an artist or a band, do not have to publish a mission statement. But its true value is that it can keep you focused on your goal, remind you of why you do what you do, and increase your chances of success. You don't have to publish it to the world, but you can certainly integrate it into your thinking.

Positioning

Positioning is the process by which you create an image or perception in the mind of your customers. It often includes competitive positioning—how your product or service is better than the competition. When I was involved with marketing high-tech products for companies such as Microsoft, Digidesign, and Cisco Systems, the subject of positioning came up almost on a daily basis. Al Ries, sometimes co-writing with Jack Trout, wrote an excellent series of books on marketing, one of them called *Positioning: the Battle for Your Mind.* Another personal favorite of mine by these two authors was (and is) *The 22 Immutable Laws of Marketing.* If you want only one book on traditional marketing techniques, *The 22 Immutable Laws of Marketing* (shown in Figure 13.5) is your best bet.

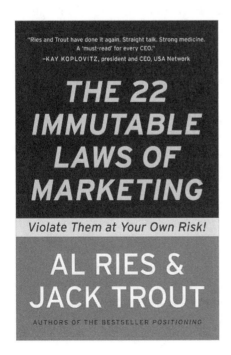

Figure 13.5
This book, by Al Ries and Jack Trout, gets my highest recommendation for understanding traditional marketing principles.

When you position a product, you define the competitive landscape in which you will compete, collect a sampling from existing customers on their perceptions of similar products in that "space," estimate the mindshare that the competitive products currently have (and how they are positioning in that space), and finally you position your product.

Your product is you or your band. Using positioning, your goal is to establish a perception of your artistry in your target market, namely, the minds of your fans. To understand who your fans are and what makes them tick, you can use a process called *market segmentation.*

Market Segmentation

The process of market segmentation enables you to focus on the precise category of prospective customers (read fans) that is most likely to purchase your offering. For large companies, this might mean dividing up the target market by size, age, sex, business function, and job responsibility. Once these qualities are defined within the target market, it's easier to zero in on the prospective customers' needs.

Perhaps the needs of your customer (music fans) are fairly straightforward—music may satisfy an emotional need that simply enhances their pleasure. The audience for music—that is, the mass market—is huge. With target marketing, you define your specific market's needs without trying to be all things to all people. What satisfies one customer, perhaps heavy metal music, might be completely inappropriate for another who likes smooth jazz. And as you know from Chapter 6, "Choosing a Video Style," on the topic of heavy metal music, that category can be further broken into many subcategories.

Your job is to know where you fall in the scheme of things and what kind of characteristics you will find in your prospective customers or fans. A lot of this occurs naturally (without requiring a lot of market research) because the qualities of your act—your music, your appearance, your message—all appeal to a specific audience in the first place. You reach your audience because you are putting forth your particular brand. If you or someone in your band is more of the analytical type, then doing some exercises in market segmentation may be worth your while.

Branding

Your exercises in positioning and market segmentation contribute to your understanding of your brand. Your brand is your identity—how you want your fans to perceive you. The degree of your success will make your brand range from unknown to a "brand name."

Naturally, everyone wants to become a brand name, a name so recognizable that no explanation is necessary to understand what that brand name represents. Examples of this are Kleenex, Fed-Ex, Amazon, Google, and The Beatles. You may not be the next Beatles, but you will want to get as high as possible on the branding ladder.

A brand might be a combination of characteristics, some of them innate, such as your body's physical appearance, and some of them created, such how you clothe that body. Often a brand has components that are intangible. And more than likely, a brand is greater than the sum of its (tangible and intangible) parts.

Have you ever seen a commercial that has absolutely nothing to do with the actual product or company? The brand is so successful that it represents a larger feeling. The brand message can be communicated without showing the product. Think Nike or Apple. There are some brands that are so strong that their (perceived) importance is much, much larger than the actual product, service, or company.

There may be more than you think when it comes to understanding the branding process, including concepts such as brand recognition, brand equity, brand franchise, and brand extension, to name a few. You can certainly succeed without this knowledge, but in a very competitive marketplace, the more you know, the better.

Value Proposition

The value proposition is one of the most corporate-sounding terms in marketing, and you may have a harder time relating to this term than to some of the others. Simply put, the *value proposition* is the statement of the sum total of benefits that your customers get for their money and/or time.

By the widest definition, you are likely to say that you provide customers with excellent entertainment. But other definitions are possible. Perhaps your band is active politically, so you provide political awareness. Perhaps your music makes people relax or brings people together in a social network. Knowing your value proposition is directly related to your positioning and, further, can make you stand out against your competition.

But most artists, let alone people in general, rarely think about this. Perhaps many people have internalized some form of a value proposition a long time ago and feel they don't need to revisit it. However, revisiting it from time to time can ensure that it reflects your value proposition as it stands today and, at the very least, brings your value proposition back into your consciousness.

One of the best ways to zero in on your specific value proposition is to see yourself from the outside. Pretend to be a potential fan at a concert looking up at the band on the stage and trying to imagine how they see you and why you stand out from other artists. If you can define your value proposition, you can broadcast that message—overly or subconsciously—to your ever-increasing audience.

The Three Ps—Public Relations, Publicity, and Promotion

PR is the "spin machine." PR (public relations) is the term most often used in the business or corporate world. Publicity is similar to PR, but is the term more common in the entertainment business. Promotion is, well, promotion. Promotion activities are activities such as trade shows, endorsements, sponsorships, and direct mail campaigns.

Although promotion may sometimes involve cash outlay, most PR activities are the type that can be executed for little or no money. If a magazine publishes a story about you as an artist, that's PR. The type of visibility that a magazine article can give you is arguably much better than if you were to take out a full-page ad in the same magazine. Indeed, this is an argument often made in debates regarding marketing budgets. Advertising is very expensive, so when budgets are tight, marketing managers (especially the ones higher up on the corporate ladder) prefer getting some free publicity to paying for full-page, four-color ads.

Some types of PR are more believable than others. One example is sponsorships. If Taylor Guitars sponsors you as an artist, people will probably think you must be a very talented performer. If they name a guitar after you and your name happens to be Taylor Swift, you probably don't need the extra publicity, but it certainly doesn't hurt! Take a look at the Taylor Guitars homepage in Figure 13.6.

The most elementary form of PR is the press release. You have probably seen press releases before, and they all follow a specific format (as indicated in the upcoming sidebar).

Press releases are written in third person, as if you were a reporter writing about the subject of the press release. In other words, you would never say, "I released my new album today." Instead, you would write, "Peter Piper released his new album today." When sending out a press release, the first thing to ask yourself is whether you really have some news. There's nothing worse than a press release that has nothing important to say. There should be some sort of story, whether it's simple, such as your new album release, or more complex, such as your new music licensing website that serves the film, television, and Internet industries.

Figure 13.6
You're doing well if you are sponsored by a company such as Taylor Guitars.
It's even sweeter if one of their guitar lines has your namesake on it.

The press release is a delicate balance between spin and fact; it's not just one or the other, but a bit of both. If the press release is written as straight spin, it will come off as hype. If it is written as pure fact, it will come off as dull. You need just enough spin to make the announcement in the press release seem exciting, as well as enough facts to substantiate your claims.

You can distribute your press release to your contacts via email. Most professionals use a press release wire service such as PR Newswire, Business Wire, or WebWire. These services do cost money, but they have a prepared list of important press contacts organized into very specific markets. You may want to research these services a bit more to see if they are something you need.

Typical Press Release Format

FOR IMMEDIATE RELEASE

This usually appears on the upper-left side of the press release and is the first indicator that this is an "official" press release.

Headline

This is one major headline (occasionally accompanied by a secondary sub-headline) similar to what you see in newspapers. The headline is designed to attract attention, but it should be factual, or it won't be believable.

City, State, Month, Day, Year

These are the first items in the first paragraph. The text of the press release immediately follows on the same line.

Main Body

This is the text of the press release in paragraph form. The first sentence summarizes the entire story and entices the readers to read more.

About (Company Information)

This is the description of the company (or individual) and what they do, and it's often reflective of the mission statement.

Contact Information

This information includes the contact person's name, company name if appropriate, phone, fax, email, physical address, and the relevant website address.

End

It is common for a press release to end with either —End— or ###. It's the official end of the press release, and there will be no doubt about it.

Advertising

Advertising is a means of getting your message out to persuade people to do something, whether it means buying your latest album or thinking that you're the best artist to come along in a century. (Be careful of that last one—advertising gives you more leeway than PR, but you still have to have your feet planted somewhere on the ground.)

Traditional advertising has relied on traditional media, including print (magazines, newspapers) broadcast television, cable television, radio, and, of course, the Internet. Advertising has grown to include any conceivable form of delivery and can now be found anywhere, from cereal boxes to sides of buses to bathroom stalls. (I didn't want to include that last one, but it demonstrates that there is no limit to what advertisers will do.)

Advertising is not cheap. A small newspaper ad can cost several thousand dollars. A television ad in prime time can cost up to $200,000, and if the commercial is run during the Super Bowl—well, I won't go there. Because advertising is expensive, it is important to measure its effectiveness. Companies have achieved this through specific telephone numbers related to a promotion or by having consumers ask about a very specific promotion. The big word here is *metrics*—that is, applying some form of measurement to the results of your advertising campaign.

Advertising in an environment such as the music business has its challenges, and never before have those challenges been as extreme as today. Because the business is undergoing such radical change, mostly as a result of the digital age and the Internet, the old forms of advertising are not as effective as they used to be. It is difficult to have a successful ad campaign in a magazine if the magazine itself is struggling for survival.

Like traditional advertising, traditional marketing has one foot in the past and a few toes in the future. The future may have more promise through social marketing, or as I stated earlier, some combination of both. So, it's time to take a close-up look at social marketing.

Social Marketing (aka Social Media Marketing)

If you were to run a search on social marketing via Google or any other search engine, the first few hits might surprise you. Some of the definitions that are cited resemble the description, almost to the letter, of the traditional marketing mix. Another site defines social marketing as the use of marketing principles that are for the greater good of society, rather than for the profits of a corporation. There are a lot more and varying definitions. Naturally, they are not the type of social marketing I'm talking about here.

Social media marketing is a much newer phenomenon than traditional marketing or even viral and guerrilla marketing. I have found that the latest, greatest thing is often overhyped

when it first emerges. It remains to be seen whether social media marketing falls into the overhyped category. Time usually tells the difference, and there hasn't been enough time yet to know for certain. Thus, my discussion of social media marketing comes with a cautionary message to use these new marketing tactics with moderation, unless of course, you are creating such a buzz that your ears won't stop ringing. In that case, keep doing what you're doing, without restraint.

The Act of Blogging

One of the first incarnations of social media marketing occurred when there was no such term as social media marketing. Blogs (a contraction of the words web and log), originally were simple logs or diaries that an individual posted on the Internet. Soon blogs also became a means of creating one's own editorial space by focusing on a particular topic and making regular entries, reporting an event or supporting an idea.

If a blog could be authored by an individual, why not have a blog authored by an individual from a particular company? Well, that's precisely what came next, with many executives, including company CEOs, writing their own blogs. The company blog accomplished several goals. It allowed a company to get its message out. The blog provided a means of creating buzz. It also created a new way to gain insight into a company's customers—to find out what they *really* think about a brand or a product.

All of these benefits apply to individuals as well, including the makers of music videos. Bands can have blogs; artists can have blogs. A band's blog may have reports from its concert tour; an artist's blog may have updates on how the latest studio recording sessions are progressing. A blog can, in short, have anything you want in it.

But the term "content is king," although overused, still has validity. Just because you can blog about something doesn't mean you should blog about it. Like other content, it needs to gain a reader's attention, have a story of some significance, and provide a reason for the readers to follow the blog.

What's the difference between a blog and a website? If you were to suppose a blog and a website have identical content, the difference is shown in the real-time experience of a blog. A blog is more immediate, timelier, and generally speaking more recent than a static website. A website needs to pull readers in. A blog pushes its contents out.

With all that in mind, it's also interesting to note that a blog can be a part of a website or a part of a MySpace page. Or it can live on its own as a blog hosted by a site specializing in blogs, such as WordPress or Blogger.com (shown in Figure 13.7).

Figure 13.7

A blog can be a part of your website or one of your social networks, or it can be on a dedicated blogging site such as Blogger.com.

An individual may blog to keep in touch with friends and relatives. A company may blog to understand and influence its customers. An artist or band may blog to increase its fan base.

Blogging is good. I highly recommend it.

The Dawn of MySpace

MySpace has been known for a long time as *the* place to go for social networking. It became a huge destination for people of all types—at first, young people looking for other young people with a desire to make friends; then professionals from all walks of life who wanted to network, promote themselves, and make friends; and ultimately, everybody and anybody had a MySpace page.

Before MySpace, anyone who wanted to create their own individual websites needed some computer programming experience. MySpace made it easy to have a "page." All you had to do was sign up.

It wasn't long until a prevalence of musicians, bands, artists, and singers seemed to dominate the MySpace population. You can sign up as an artist/musician and have your own space to upload your original music, play it, sell it, announce your touring schedule, create a blog, and in every way, shape, and form promote yourself until the cows come home. And perhaps most important of all, you can upload ten of your own original tracks for people to listen to or download. In Figure 13.8, you can see my main MySpace page with the music player on the right.

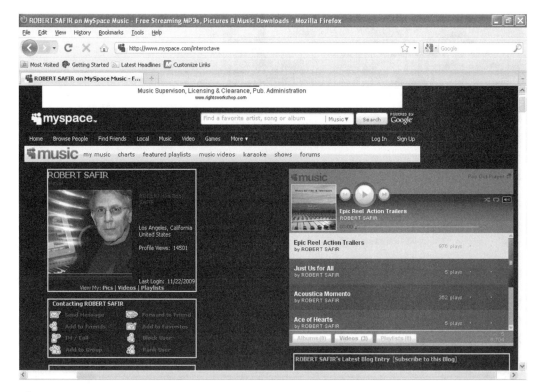

Figure 13.8
This is my MySpace page showing the music player on the right.

The naysayers would always point out, however, that nobody ever came up through the ranks for real pop music visibility by having a MySpace page. That's no longer true, and one example, among many, is Kate Voegele, seen in Figure 13.9. She, and other artists, went from relative obscurity to high visibility by way of MySpace.

Figure 13.9
Kate Voegele, shown here on the MySpace Records page, is one of several successful independent artists who emerged from MySpace.com.

But what goes up must come down, as they say. Once the darling of online social sites, MySpace has lost favor and market share to others, such as Facebook. Once upon a time you *had to have* a MySpace page. Now you have to have a Facebook page.

The one huge exception to this is MySpace Music. The management at MySpace realized that they could leverage their huge population of music makers and music lovers into nothing less than their own label, which they formed in 2005 as a joint venture with Interscope Records. Today, MySpace has positioned itself as a social networking site that specializes or focuses on music, with its own label, MySpace Records.

MySpace Records is the label. However, label aside, there is a Music *page* on MySpace at www.music.myspace.com, shown in Figure 13.10. The Music page includes Music Videos, music video Charts, News, Shows & Events, Playlists, Artist's Activity, and a whole lot more. Music playlists can be selected from categories such as Major, Indie, Unsigned, or Recently added by Friends.

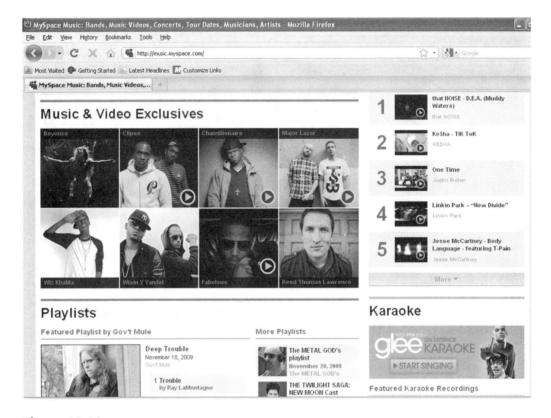

Figure 13.10
Not to be confused with MySpace Records, the record label, is the music page on MySpace, known as MySpace Music.

There is also a Music Video page that features staff picks, hot videos, and recent videos (categorized by artists your friends are watching and artists you're watching). Figure 13.11 shows the MySpace Video page with a video of Beyonce currently playing.

So, what you might be wondering is how you can be featured on MySpace Music (and ultimately, how you can get your music video featured on the Music Video page).

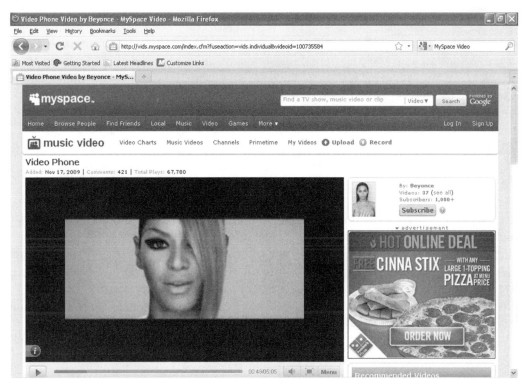

Figure 13.11
A specific channel for music videos is in the Video section on the MySpace site.

What MySpace Says About Becoming a Featured Artist on the MySpace Music Page

How does MySpace choose featured artists, musicians, and comedians? We're totally committed to celebrating the best in music, art, and comedy. We get really excited when we discover new talent and get to showcase their work! Just so you know, we don't accept artist requests for feature coverage, since we prefer to leave it to the MySpace community to decide.

When we see a lot of traffic on an artist profile, we check it out. If there's a good buzz, we sometimes give them a shout out.

Well, if you mean the label, MySpace Music, you would have been noticed by now and signed a contract with MySpace/Interscope. But as an artist, how do you get featured on the MySpace Music page? Unfortunately, it's not up to *you*. The answer is not unlike the method of climbing up the "charts" at YouTube—you have to have traffic, tons of traffic, coming to your own MySpace page. Then you get noticed (by MySpace staff). If you have enough "buzz" about you or the band, you may hear from a MySpace staffer.

What applies to music applies to music videos. You need to build up enough traffic to your own page before you can become a featured artist or have a highly visible music video on MySpace. But in the meantime, you need to get your music video on your main page and use every tool you can to build traffic. This means not only having your music video easily visible on your page (I've got my videos visible right on my main page as shown in Figure 13.12), but also using every method you can to build awareness. The tasks are the ones I've been discussing—post your music and your music videos, create a blog, and "friend" people (yes, *friend* is a verb now, as is *unfriend*). Post your touring schedule or appearances, get involved in groups, and use the bulletin board to make announcements that go out to your list of friends.

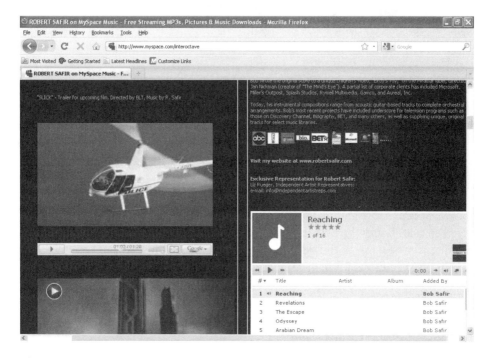

Figure 13.12
Make sure your own video is easily accessible on your main MySpace page, as illustrated here on my MySpace page.

Finally, network (or friend) with the type of people you would want to hang out with or get to know on a professional level. Those people might be your peers—other artists or bands. They might also be the managers, agents, or independent labels you would like to work with. But here's a word of caution—don't throw yourself at your music business connections and plead with them to visit your page. Such behavior comes off as desperate. It ignores the fact that these particular contacts also have a life, and probably a very busy one. Sure, you want them to visit your page. But use other methods, such as social skills (even if they are actually *online* social skills) to get people interested enough to hear your music and see your music video.

One of the coolest new features of MySpace is the Artist Dashboard. This dashboard provides you with statistics on your page views, the total songs played, the songs played today, other song statistics including trends, and the demographics of your audience. A summary of your dashboard appears on the page in which you manage your profile, as shown in Figure 13.13. Clicking View All Stats in the lower-right corner brings you to the complete dashboard page, shown in Figure 13.14.

The Artist Dashboard comes complete with charts and graphs, and it's free. This is the equivalent of having an analyst (not a shrink, but a number cruncher) on your personal payroll. Use these statistics to understand who your audience is, what tracks they like, and what these numbers and charts show about trends relative to your music. You might consider these facts before you choose which song to transform into a music video; and if you've already done that, consider the Artist Dashboard as a resource for determining what video to make next time.

Figure 13.13

The summary of the Artist Dashboard appears when you manage your main page after signing in.

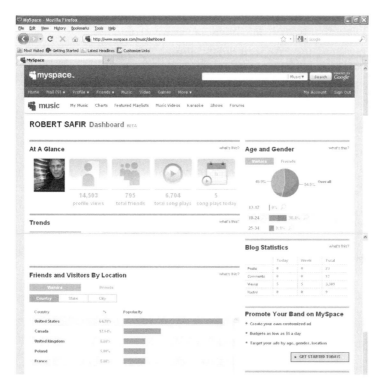

Figure 13.14
Clicking on View All Stats on the Artist Dashboard summary brings you to this page,
loaded with statistics that can be useful in understanding your audience.

iLike iMeem

Ahh, for the love of acronyms, there has to be a joke in here, somewhere. But what
is no joke is the rapidity in which the music landscape changes. As of this writing,
the formerly independent and mostly alternative sites, iLike and iMeem, were individual companies. But now they have been acquired by MySpace. Among MySpace
Music, iLike, and iMeem, it's not yet clear what long-term strategy lives in the minds
of MySpace music execs. Streaming, downloading, purchasing, and subscribing, or
any combination of these is certainly possible. What it means for music videos is
more uncertain, as the focus of iLike and iMeem has been more about audio and
less about video. Time will tell, and by the time you read this book, the music landscape might be quite different than it is now.

For MySpace to work for you, you must be involved and active with it. If you do that, you can increase your traffic. If you increase your traffic, you increase the likelihood that your music video will be seen, and that your career just might take off.

The Rise of Facebook

Facebook's rapid rise in popularity has led it to a position no one could have predicted in the early days of MySpace domination. Facebook is now the "Hertz Cars" of the social

networking sites, whereas MySpace has become the "Avis" of the bunch. Translated into plain English, in case you haven't seen a lot of television commercials for Hertz or Avis, Facebook is now number one, whereas MySpace is number two.

One of the main features of Facebook is the Wall, where you and your Facebook friends can post messages for others to see. You also can upload photos, share information via News Feed, update your Status, and gently Poke a friend who usually Pokes you in kind. You can join networks, form groups, and search for and add new friends to your heart's content. These are all features you can access and change via your Home Page or Profile Page. See my Profile Page in Figure 13.15 (as you can see in the figure, Facebook Pages tend to be text-oriented and not as graphic as some social sites).

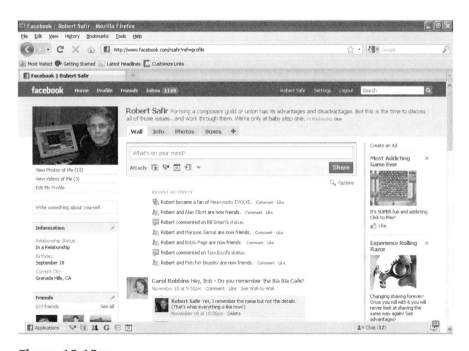

Figure 13.15
Here is my Profile Page on Facebook.

Facebook also lets you upload videos. Your video is compressed and converted into a Flash file that plays right on your Profile Page. This is one way to put your music video out there, but it's not the only way.

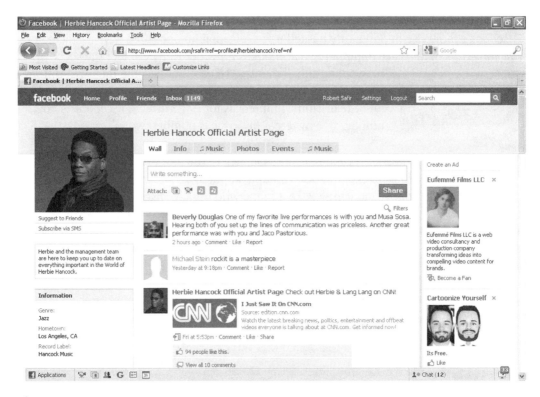

Figure 13.16
Herbie Hancock's Page on Facebook.

What may be of more importance to you as an artist and music video producer is the Facebook feature known as Pages. Pages allow Facebook members to become a fan of a product, a service, or an individual. (Herbie Hancock has a Page as a professional artist, shown in Figure 13.16.) You might think of a Facebook Page as a commercial version of a regular Facebook account. And speaking of commercial, if you have a Page, you are also able to advertise, using pay-per-click or pay-per-impression advertising rates. As an advertiser, you get access to real-time reporting and other statistical results related to your ad.

Online Advertising Rates

There is a lot to learn if you want to pursue online advertising (whether on Facebook, Google, or anywhere else). In brief, here are a couple of terms you ought to know:

▷ **PPC:** With pay-per-click, you pay only when your ad is clicked on.

▷ **CPC:** Cost-per-click is what you pay if there is "click-through," meaning when visitors click on an ad that results in them visiting your website.

▷ **Flat-rate and bid-based PPC:** Rates for PPC can be based on a fixed flat rate, or they can be bid on. You name the price, but the highest bidder's (meaning your competitors who are also price-bidding) results are displayed first.

▷ **CPM:** Cost-per-thousand, based on views (cost per thousand views). This is part of the pay-per-impression model.

The topic of online advertising covers huge territory. Click-through rate, cost-per-click, cost-per-impression, and conversation rate are just a few of the terms you'll discover if you pursue online advertising. Perhaps the best known of all online advertising concepts is Google AdWords, in which you choose keywords relative to your business. When users search on these keywords, your ad will come up next to Google's search results.

Although it is possible to upload videos to a regular Facebook account and to upload music-only tracks using several third-party apps available through Facebook, the Pages option allows more professional-looking results. You will find Pages from some of the music industry's most popular artists on Facebook Pages.

Using Facebook Pages does *not* require you to participate in online advertising. The basic concept of Pages and fans helps to spread your message virally. When a fan interacts with your Page, stories linking to your Page can be directed via News Feed to *their* friends. When these friends interact with your Page, the News Feed keeps spreading the word, via word-of-mouth, to a wider network of friends.

You can do many things on a Facebook Page that you cannot do on a regular Profile Page. Figure 13.17 shows how you can Browse or Search for a specific artists. (You can see how the "King of Pop" appears at the very top of the list.) Figure 13.18 shows U2's Video section selected from its artist Page. A professional Page enables you to host numerous videos from a central location as opposed to scattered videos showing up on a Wall or Newsfeed on a "regular" Page.

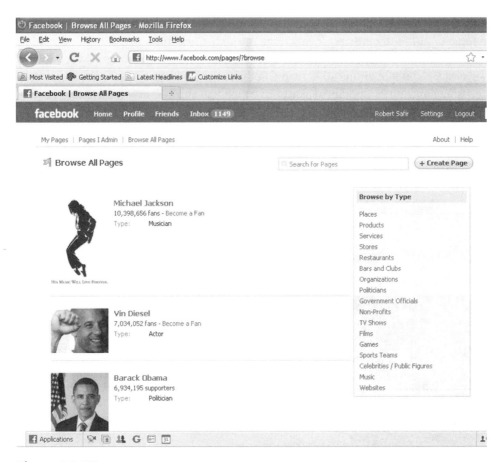

Figure 13.17
You can use Facebook's Browse and Search functions to locate specific artists.

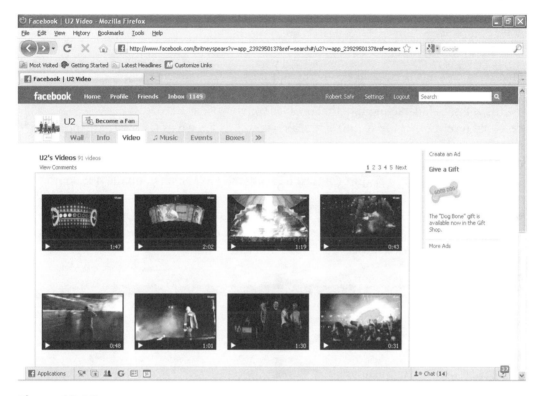

Figure 13.18
Shown here is U2's Video section from its artist Page.

You also have the capability to send out messages to fans by clicking Send Update to Friends. This can be any kind of announcement, sales promotion, or news of an upcoming concert or event.

Facebook is in a very good position in the social-marketing landscape. How all of the competition in this landscape plays out remains to be seen. From your perspective, as an artist and music video maker, you need to keep on top of the fast-moving developments that occur in social media marketing. There are always two fronts to keep track of: the social media sites available to the public and the sites (social or not) that are focused on the music business. Those are your playgrounds.

Using Twitter and Tweets

"Twitter and tweets" sounds like something from a Warner Brothers cartoon, but it's no joking matter. Twitter is a social-marketing tool that enables you to send and receive short (up to 140 characters) messages known as *tweets.* These messages can travel by a number of means, including the Twitter website, email, text messaging, and instant messaging. Tweets started out as simple updates on what you were doing at any given moment, such as "just combed hair, listening to Mariah C. on the 405 south." (Within this message are a couple of potential social problems —combing one's hair while driving is one of them, as is sending a text message while on the freeway. But that's another topic altogether.) There are a few *million* tweets posted every day by over a million users. Figure 13.19 shows just a few tweets from a moment in time.

Figure 13.19
With Twitter, you can follow updates on what people are doing—and they can follow you.

Although tweets began life as simple messages about a person's status, it wasn't long before people realized that they could use it for more commercial purposes, such as sharing information about their products or services. Short electronic messages of any kind are sometimes grouped under the heading of "microblogs" or status updates (which is also one of the features on MySpace or Facebook).

Twitter is no longer considered a simple, personal message service for the under-30 crowd. It has grown to be used in a vast number of ways, including the following:

▷ Promotion

▷ Advertising

▷ Surveys

▷ Emergencies

▷ Political campaigns

▷ News

Twitter was even used as a communication platform during a Shuttle mission to service the Hubble Telescope.

Many people question and debate the viability of Twitter for any purpose beyond casual conversation. Can Twitter really be used as a marketing tool? You can, in fact, use tweets to:

▷ Send out updates about your band.

▷ Promote special offers such as CDs on sale.

▷ Link to news pages (or for that matter, any page) on your own website.

▷ Create buzz.

▷ Reinforce your brand as an artist or band.

If you decide to use Twitter, make sure you get familiar with Twitter etiquette and the proper format for creating tweets. In general, it's a good idea to keep the tone informal, conversational, and personal. This is not your father's advertising vehicle. Try to be less "in-your-face" and more "hey, check this out."

Visit Us, Follow Us, Join Us

The Internet has given you an easy way to spread your message, above and beyond a specific site in which you choose to participate. Now, in the form of buttons, badges, or plain old links, you can be an electronic Johnny Appleseed. You do this in the form of placing these badges everywhere in which you have a presence, such as "Visit us on Facebook" (or MySpace or YouTube Channel, and so on). An example of these buttons can be seen in Figure 13.20.

It's the easiest, quickest form of cross-marketing ever developed. Use it wisely and frequently.

Figure 13.20
Everyone can find everyone else with badges or buttons. You can find them, visit them, and follow them. Just try not to annoy them.

About LinkedIn

I wanted to briefly mention LinkedIn, which is more of a business-oriented social networking site. It allows you to establish a link of contacts or *connections,* which through the laws of mathematics, continue over time to expand your network of additional contacts. LinkedIn can be used to make contact with people you wouldn't ordinarily be able to reach (in the boring, mundane physical world) and can even be used to find or announce information about jobs or business opportunities.

LinkedIn also features groups. Anyone can form these groups, and just about anyone can join one, the main requirement being that you are actually a member of a certain community or discipline. There is a place in which you can provide answers to questions posed by other LinkedIn members, which is an opportunity to show your expertise in a particular subject. You can drive members to your own blog, and you can link to your own website.

LinkedIn may not be the ideal place for an up-and-coming band or artist, at least in terms of building a fan base. However, as a business-oriented site, you may find it useful in other ways, such as connecting with agents, managers, publicists, record labels, and so on. You will also find ways to connect to colleagues—other artists, songwriters, and musicians. Think of LinkedIn as social network for the business aspects of your career, and the other social sites I discussed as social-marketing sites to connect you with and build up your fan base.

Using Other Marketing Methods

A variety of marketing methods can be viewed as a part of both traditional and social media. They are as follows (in no particular order):

▷ **Email blasts:** Sending emails to a list has origins in the corporate world. You can use email blasts to promote events to your fans or news to the music industry. I'd just advise you not to overdo this method and to give people an opportunity to opt out of receiving your messages.

▷ **Links to and from other sites:** You may find sites where you'd like to have some sort of presence. Perhaps the site would be interested in having a presence on your website. Trading links is the way to accomplish this, which you do by identifying the best contact on the site you're interested in and suggesting cross-linking. If it becomes a done deal, the links can be in the form of a URL or a button, a banner, or even a photo or video.

▷ **Trading banner ads:** As in the preceding case, an appropriate or relevant trade of banner ads might be a possibility. It's a lot cheaper than having to purchase a banner ad. Keep in mind though that the once glorious world of banner advertising is not as attractive or welcomed as it once was.

▷ **Optimized search:** Learn what you need to do to include important keywords about you or your band so that you will come up often in search engine results. There is both a science and an art to this, and search engine optimization (SEO) is the subject of many books and articles.

▷ **Landing pages:** These are pages that you specifically build on your own website, usually to measure the results of a particular marketing campaign. Say, for example, that you are giving free T-shirts away to the first 25 fans who respond to a contest question. The question may be located on your homepage or anywhere on the Internet. The thing to do is to have respondents go to a specific URL or landing page on your site where you can measure the number of respondents to this promotion.

▷ **Contests, promotions, and give-aways:** These are fairly self-explanatory. But as with landing pages, make sure you have a way to measure the results. Otherwise, you won't know where to put your time and energy to promote yourself.

▷ **Web analytics:** Measuring traffic on your landing page is one thing, but analyzing traffic on your site—from where people enter the site to which pages they usually migrate to—can tell you a lot about the overall effectiveness of your web design. Google provides some tools for this for free, and several software companies make applications specifically designed for this purpose.

▷ **Internet forums:** Participating in Internet forums is another way to have a presence and to get additional insight as to what other people (including fans) are thinking. You can have a forum of your own making as well as participate in relevant forums that already exist.

And the Winner Is…

In the beginning of this chapter, I discussed two different schools of thought—traditional marketing and social marketing, with ardent believers on each end of the spectrum. Today, there is no shortage of blogs on which one is better than the other.

Many people refer to social marketing as *relationship marketing.* Perhaps social marketing, with an emphasis on relationships, has been the missing ingredient in traditional marketing. Or, just to make your head buzz, maybe it is traditional marketing that has been missing from social marketing. People will continue to debate the effectiveness of traditional marketing and social-media marketing. As I have stated, I believe a blend of both approaches works best. Your mileage may vary, but keep an open mind when you begin your marketing efforts and see where that takes you. Usually surprises are in store.

Finding a Formula for Fool-Proof Marketing

If you'd like a fool-proof method of marketing your music video on the Internet, you may have to look elsewhere—and you may have to look for a long, long time. None of the methods discussed here are guarantees of anything. Nor is there an absolute formula for which marketing methods, and in what combination, you should use. A lot of it comes from trial and error. But if your experimentation is built on some basic knowledge of marketing techniques—old school and new school—your chances of success are greatly increased.

Enjoy the Ultimate in Creativity

When you stop and think about it, creating a music video—from beginning to end—and marketing it by using the Internet—has to be one of the most creative endeavors in which you can engage. A tremendous amount of creativity is necessary in every aspect of this process—creating the music, visualizing the story, producing the video, and creating and executing a marketing strategy. You can act on your imagination to take your ideas further with less cost than ever before, due in great part to the advances in technology that we enjoy today.

A tremendous amount of learning takes place during this process. Even if your effort doesn't produce ultimate success your first time out, the experience of creating and marketing your music video will benefit you the next time and the next time after that.

As a maker of music videos, you practice many disciplines and are "many people," all rolled into one. You are a songwriter. You are a film director. You are a marketing director. You are an entrepreneur.

You are a producer and a consumer—the ultimate *prosumer*—engaged in an exciting and tremendously creative endeavor.

Learning to make music videos is a combination of knowledge and experience, with a heavy emphasis on the latter. I often read about filmmakers who began using 8mm or 16mm film as a child and making their first movies when they could barely hold the camera. My choice was Super-8. Even back then, I used a primitive splicing block and something resembling Scotch Tape for my first attempts at film editing.

So I say, if you are not sure whether to make a music video based upon some wild idea spinning around in your head—make it.

If you're not sure whether to make a music video based upon a song you have sitting on the shelf—make it.

If you're not sure whether you should make an effort in music video-making because you might fail at it—make it. Make it anyway. Mistakes will be the lessons you can apply next time, and success may be just one of many more music video productions to come. Either way, you will have a lot of fun.

Enjoy.

Resources

I T MIGHT SEEM ODD AT FIRST to have an appendix with a section called "Books on Social Change," but if you have read some of this book, you've already seen how social transformation has changed the music business and in turn, the making of music videos.

The appendix also lists resources related to Logic. This is because my most recent experience is with Logic, but in no way does this infer that Logic must be your workstation of choice. Almost any digital audio workstation (DAW) available on the market today will provide you with the digital tools you need for music video creation.

I sincerely hope that some of the resources listed here will be of value to you.

Short List of Relevant Course PTR Books

I've compiled a short list of a few Course PTR books that go into more depth on some of the topics discussed in this book, including music, audio, film, video, plug-ins, and more.

▷ *Audio Post-Production in Your Project Studio* by Casey Kim (ISBN-10: 1598634194, 2008)

▷ *Myspace for Musicians* by Fran Vincent (ISBN-10: 1435454197; 2011)

▷ *Logic Pro 8 Power!* by Orren Merton/Kevin Anker (ISBN-10: 1598633694; 2009)

▷ *Going Pro with Logic Pro 8* by Jay Asher (ISBN-10: 1598635611; 2009)

▷ *Apple Final Cut Pro 6* by Lisa Rysinger (ISBN-10: 1401877915; 2009)

Books on Traditional Marketing

These are great books on marketing and easy reads as well. *The Tipping Point,* while not technically a marketing book, lends a lot to the general understanding of marketing.

▷ *The 22 Immutable Laws of Marketing* by Al Ries and Jack Trout (ISBN-10: 0887306667; 1994)

▷ *The 11 Immutable Laws of Internet Branding* by Al Ries and Laura Ries (ISBN-10: 0060196211; 2000)

▷ *The Tipping Point: How Little Things Can Make a Big Difference* by Malcolm Gladwell (ISBN-10: 0316346624; 2002)

Books on Social Change

Alvin Toffler and Marshall McLuhan wrote the first editions of their books a long time ago, yet the principles they put forth are still as valid today as they were then.

▷ *Future Shock* by Alvin Toffler (ISBN-10: 0553277375; 1984)

▷ *The Third Wave* by Alvin Toffler (ISBN-10: 0553246984; 1984)

▷ *Understanding Media* by Marshall McLuhan (ISBN-10: 0262631598; 1994)

▷ *The Global Village* by Marshall McLuhan (ISBN-10: 0195079108; 1992)

Music—Educational and Informational

Course PTR has many books covering music technology, film, and video, all of which can be found on its website. Artist House Music has many educational videos in addition to its articles. The last two gentlemen in this section are experts on songwriting and the music business, respectively.

▷ www.courseptr.com

▷ www.artistshousemusic.com

▷ www.johnbraheny.com

▷ www.donpassman.com

Websites that Host Video

Some of these are general sites that also host video (such as YouTube), whereas others are more video-specific.

▷ www.youtube.com

▷ www.mtv.com

▷ www.vh1.com

▷ www.veoh.com

▷ www.vimeo.com

▷ www.radarmusicvideos.com

▷ www.dailymotion.com

▷ www.blip.tv

▷ www.photobucket.com

Social Networking Websites

There are too many social networking websites to mention (and new ones are popping up all the time), so I'll keep the focus on the ones I mentioned in this book.

▷ www.myspace.com

▷ www.facebook.com

▷ www.twitter.com

▷ www.linkedin.com

▷ www.blogger.com

- ▷ www.iMeem.com
- ▷ www.iLike.com
- ▷ www.bebo.com

Manufacturers Websites

A comprehensive list would be very long, but the two that I put at the top of the list are Apple (for QuickTime, Final Cut, Logic, iTunes, iMovie, and so on) and Sorenson because of its quality codecs.

- ▷ www.apple.com
- ▷ www.sorenson.com

Film and Television Business Websites

IMDb stands for Internet Movie Database (and is actually owned by Amazon). Everyone associated with every film or television show can be found there. Actors Access and LA Casting are sites that can help you find talent for your music video.

- ▷ www.imdb.com
- ▷ www.actorsaccess.com
- ▷ www.lacasting.com

Websites About Websites

Alexa can give you the stats on any website you enter. (Try entering the name of your own website.) Search Engine Watch can teach you a lot about SEO and SEM (including what those acronyms stand for).

- ▷ www.alexa.com
- ▷ www.searchenginewatch.com

Website of the Greatest Music Instrument Catalog on Earth

Need I say more?

- ▷ www.sweetwater.com

Index

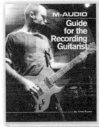

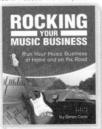

COURSE TECHNOLOGY
CENGAGE Learning
Professional • Technical • Reference

Course Technology PTR

COURSE CLIPS

Introducing *Course Clips*!

Course Clips are interactive DVD-ROM training products for those who prefer learning on the computer as opposed to learning through a book. *Course Clips Starters* are for beginners and *Course Clips Masters* are for more advanced users.

Pro Tools 8
Course Clips Master
Steve Wall ■ $49.99

Pro Tools 8
Course Clips Starter
Steve Wall ■ $29.99

Ableton Live 8
Course Clips Master
Brian Jackson ■ $49.99